FILM TITLE SEQUENCES: A CRITICAL ANTHOLOGY

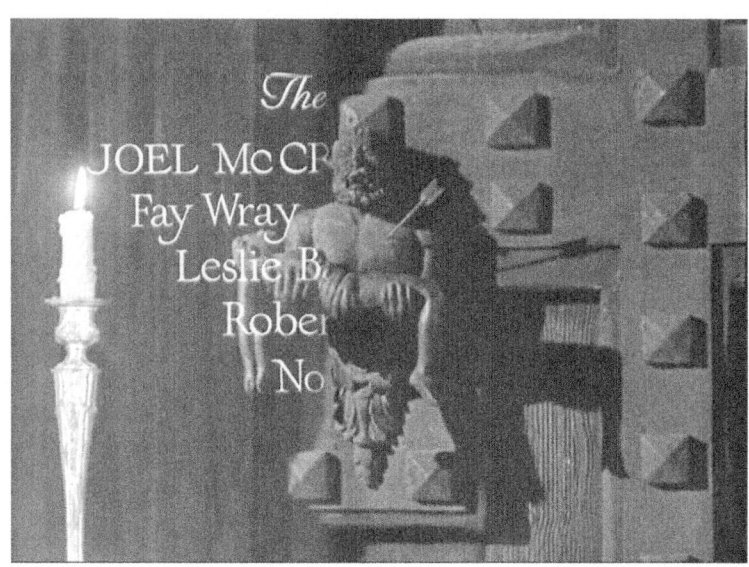

The Most Dangerous Game (1932)

Film Title Sequences

A Critical Anthology

Deborah Allison

Pilea Publications
London

First published by Pilea Publications, London, 2021

The front cover artwork pays homage to the work of two giants of film title sequence design: Maurice Binder and Saul Bass.

CONTENTS

FOREWORD

I first became hooked on film title sequences in the early 1990s, and started to collect them in 1995. Back in those dark ages, this entailed diligent scouring of the weekly television guide and a socially ruinous enslavement to the broadcast schedules as I sat poised in front of a VHS recorder trying to catch near-simultaneous title sequences on different channels. To make matters worse, a 4:3 television aspect ratio meant that many sequences were severely cropped, squeezed, or 'panned and scanned'.

The subsequent advent of widescreen television, DVD, Blu-ray, broadband internet, and streaming services has made life a great deal easier for title sequence enthusiasts and has encouraged a growing interest in the history of title design. It is now possible to watch many of the sequences discussed in this book (and plenty of others besides) with remarkable ease—and usually in the correct ratio. There are several websites devoted to title sequences, among which you can currently find good collections of clips and stills housed at *Art of the Title* (artofthetitle.com), *Title Design Project* (titledesignproject.com), *Movie Title*

Stills Collection (annyas.com/screenshots), and *Watch the Titles!* (watchthetitles.com).

The first writing output based on my own slowly and painfully assembled collection was my 2001 doctoral thesis, *Promises in the Dark: Opening Title Sequences in American Feature Films of the Sound Period*. Once upon a time, I had plans to adapt it into a book but, as so often happens, other commitments and projects got in the way. My fascination with title sequences remains undiminished, nonetheless, and this has led to a string of shorter publications over the years. They are now of sufficient number and range that I felt there would be some value in bringing them together here.

Each essay in this volume was written as a stand-alone piece, so I hope you will forgive the reiteration of some key points, especially within the introductory paragraphs. I've endeavoured to arrange the essays into a sensible order, rather than placing them in the order in which they first appeared. As they cover an 18-year span, any uses of such words as 'recent' should be taken in context. Details of original publication can be found at the end of each essay.

I have resisted the inevitable urge to rewrite bits of the older essays, but I have made a few other adjustments in the service of formatting consistency—standardising spelling and citation style, and adding the names of film directors to essays from which they were formerly absent. Aside from the correction of occasional typos, any other minor differences from the original publications are accidental. I am grateful to all the various editors who showed their faith in these essays and were the first to let them loose on the world, and to Vic Pratt for proofing this anthology and much, much more.

Deborah Allison, June 2021

FIRST THINGS FIRST

"The beginning is the most important part of the work", argued Socrates in Plato's *Republic*. More than two millennia later we find in popular cinematic practice a continued proof of the sagacity of his claim. A film's opening moments act both as a declaration of intent that can shape audience expectations for better or for worse and as a pledge that those viewers will expect to be honoured. With this in mind, most filmmakers have been keen to captivate and entertain their audiences from the very start.

Throughout most of the history of cinema, for reasons owing more to business than pleasure, one of the very first things to appear on screen has been a list of credits. The most famous names can in themselves, of course, serve as promises of gratification to come; but it didn't take filmmakers long to discover the benefits of using image and, later, sound to liven up a potentially dull list of names while edging viewers into an appropriate humour for receiving their film. Looking back on the ways that the most popular styles of title sequence have differed over time we can observe a series of artistic changes which reflect a shift away from the conception of credits themselves as the sole purpose of opening title sequences and towards one which recognises the more wide-ranging potential of these first moments.

Like the movies themselves, title sequences had modest beginnings. As far back as 1897, motion picture producers began to recognise the prudence of protecting their copyright through the inclusion of their name or logo. In the earliest stages, the ways in which they did so did not constitute title sequences in the way that we think of them now, however. The American film entrepreneur Thomas Edison, for instance, began by placing his name on a strip of film just two inches long. On screen for merely a fraction of a second, this credit would have barely been visible to audiences; quite clearly it was not designed to be seen by them. Other producers—most notably the French illusionist George Méliès—placed their company logos in far more visible places, painting them right onto their film sets so that they popped up from time to time in the most unexpected places! Yet, while the extratextual information that we now associate with opening title sequences had nineteenth-century roots, it was not until other changes had occurred in film form and movie marketing that title sequences as we have come to know them began to emerge.

Actors and writers were the first contracted members of the production crew to gain on-screen credit, clearly reflecting the move towards the star-centred, narrative filmmaking style that came to dominate American cinema in the 1910s and beyond. G. M. Anderson, star of the 'Broncho Billy' films, was credited on screen from 1908 (the first actor to be so distinguished, according to *Guinness*); actors' names began to appear on film posters from 1909; and, by the following year, the crediting of actors, both on-screen and off, had become standard practice. In this way, the fledgling star system responded to and fortified audience enthusiasm for particular performers, seeking to cultivate actor recognition and thereby secure a powerful tool for marketing their later pictures.

It was around this time that the motion picture industry began to move away from catering primarily to downmarket nickelodeons and to reposition itself as a business whose product could attract more educated and affluent (and therefore lucrative) cinemagoers. A shift towards longer and more sophisticated narratives would prove central to this process. As writers took on an increasingly important role through this decade, their names began to appear on the front of the picture with increasingly regularity. It was a move designed to court the involvement of established novelists and playwrights as much as it signalled the films' 'credibility' to middle-class audiences.

By the late 1910s, feature length narrative films had become the norm, the studio system was entering full swing, and trade unions were becoming increasingly organised and powerful. The changing composition of film crews and the industrial context in which they worked provoked an escalation in the number of on-screen credits. As the litany of names grew so did design creativity and with this came the development of title sequences as multifunctional introductions. Through the 1920s, title cards illustrated with appropriate imagery became more common, while a small proportion demonstrated considerable technical ingenuity in the form of topical special effects.

This trend for eye-catching openings would gather speed through the course of the 1930s when a select group of films were heralded by a host of visual delights. *Haunted Gold* (Mack V. Wright, 1932), a Western in which a mysterious rider helps a cowboy protect a goldmine from bandits, opens with the arresting image of an ominous, cloaked silhouette from whose heart a volley of black bats fly out towards the camera. The upbeat musical *Flying Down to Rio* (Thornton Freedland, 1933) also starts in lively fashion as a plane flies toward the camera until it is so close that only its whirring propellers are framed, dissolving thereupon to a spinning main title card. A variation on a classic trick titling effect can be found in the family-friendly shipwreck saga *Captains Courageous* (Victor Fleming, 1937) where the titles appear upon wooden boards resembling a section from a boat's hull. At the end of each title card a big wave splashes up over the screen with an audible crash, wiping to a new set of titles as water pours down the boards. In contrast to these, Warner Bros.' heavyweight social drama, *They Won't Forget* (Mervyn Le Roy, 1937) promises no such fun and starts as it will continue, in grandiloquent style, tilting down from the sky to a main title apparently spelled from letter-shaped mountains in the middle of a broad plain and whose ostensibly gargantuan size is suggested by artificially exaggerated perspective.

In such films as these we can see that, whatever technique is used, each title sequence helps to set the tone for the film that will follow—a strategy that was generally applied with equal diligence in the far larger number of less ambitious sequences that contented themselves with still images. The same is true of the many sequences that followed the earlier vogue for plain or simple abstract backgrounds and which signalled the film's genre, setting, theme, or sensibility purely through choice of typeface and musical style.

Through the course of the 1940s, extravagant novelty techniques fell out of favour while another very different trend began to emerge. It was one which would prove to have far greater long-term significance, anticipating the

They Won't Forget (1937)

style of title sequence most pervasive in the contemporary cinema. Instead of maintaining a clear demarcation between the opening title sequence and the film 'proper', filmmakers began to blur this boundary by presenting diegetic and, increasingly, narrative material underneath the titles. In the 1940s it was rare for any significant action to occur during the title sequence, although series of location shots, travelling horse riders or vehicles, and so forth, became more and more common. *Deadline at Dawn* (Harold Clurman, 1940), *The Immortal Sergeant* (John M. Stahl, 1943), and *The Fugitive* (John Ford, 1947) are just a few films which introduce characters during the opening titles. By the final years of the 1950s at least two thirds of title sequences would involve some sort of diegetic material, about half of those entailing characters engaged in activity relevant to the story, although the widespread adoption of sound effects and dialogue would prove a much slower process.

The 1950s would, famously, bring another interesting development, however. Until this point, the vast majority of title sequences had been designed anonymously, often by the staff of large companies such as Pacific Title which specialised in this kind of work. In 1954, director Otto Preminger invited Saul Bass, who came from a very different professional background, to design first the publicity materials and then a title sequence for his latest picture, *Carmen Jones*. An art school-educated graphic designer who had worked extensively in advertising (and who, over the years would design some of the world's most famous corporate logos, including AT&T, Warner Communications, and Quaker Oats), Bass brought in ideas from the advertising world. In particular, his work was associated with the idea of 'key art', which involved the selection of one very simple motif to represent the product—in this case, the coming film. Acclaimed by audiences and critics alike, Bass's prolific output of title sequences for Preminger, Alfred Hitchcock, and others would come to be widely emulated. In the late 1950s and 1960s and through into the 1970s a relatively small but fondly remembered string of films would open with stylish, attention-grabbing graphics by a new wave of auteur-designers. Amongst the others to establish names for themselves during this period were Maurice Binder, Pablo Ferro, Wayne Fitzgerald, Richard Kuhn, and Don Record.

Yet just as title design of the 1940s had responded to the perceived excesses of some sequences of the previous decade, so in the late 1970s the pendulum would swing away from ostentatious graphics once again. These years would instead further the long-dominant stylistic trend toward title sequences which featured images and narrative material that segued easily into the main part of the film. The 1980s would, for the most part, follow suit although, with many films moving the bulk of their ever-growing credits roll to the end of the picture, a significant number reverted to the long-abandoned technique of a few brief opening titles upon an entirely plain background. This time round there would be a notable difference, though: the emergence of computer graphics encouraged new kinds of experimentation with animated credit lettering such as the abstract formations observable in *The Terminator* (James Cameron, 1984).

The Terminator (1984)

In recent years, digital capabilities have come to play an ever more important role in title design as they have in cinema more broadly. In particular, sequences designed by the company Imaginary Forces and its founding director Kyle Cooper, such as *The Island of Dr. Moreau* (John Frankenheimer, 1996), *Mimic* (Guillermo del Toro, 1997), and *Spider-Man* (Sam Raimi, 2002), helped to bring complex and eye-catching sequences back to the forefront of title design. Now, even while a growing number of films are choosing to forego opening titles entirely in favour of an immediate launch into the main action, the coincidence of a steady flow of skilful and innovative new sequences, a burgeoning critical interest in the history of the form, and an increased level of access to a wide range of older pieces through freely available online streaming looks set to ensure the future of opening title sequences as a potent device by which to welcome viewers to the film experience.

First published in *Schnitt*, issue 55 (2009), 8–11, in German translation from the English-language original.

BEYOND SAUL BASS: A CENTURY OF AMERICAN FILM TITLE SEQUENCES

Back in 1928, Herbert C. McKay wrote a filmmaking manual which offered the following advice: "The main title group with the first title may be made as elaborate as one desires as few spectators stop to read them anyway aside from the simple title of the film."[1] During the many decades that have passed since then, countless filmmakers have risen to this challenge. In doing so they have discovered an enormous range of ways in which to engage their audiences during the time in which the credit titles appear. From the elaborate novelty work of *Maytime* (Tay Garnett, 1937) to the elegant but striking compositions of *Three Godfathers* (John Ford, 1948), and from Friz Freleng's playfully self-reflexive animation for *The Pink Panther* (Blake Edwards, 1963) to Richard Morrison's deliciously macabre prelude to *Sweeney Todd* (Tim Burton, 2007), filmmakers have found numerous methods by which to entertain us during the opening credits and to whet our appetite for the film to come.

It would seem that scholarly interest in film title sequences is flourishing at present, if the dozens of students emailing me in relation to their dissertations can be considered any measure. At the same time, the current popular understanding of titling history has a lot of catching up to do. Until very recently (indeed, still today) talking and writing about title sequences has almost invariably gravitated towards the work of a handful of acclaimed designers such as Saul Bass, Maurice Binder, and Kyle Cooper. This auteurist focus—propagated by newspapers and websites, as well as a range of semi-academic magazines and journals—has given rise to some significant misconceptions about the history of film titling, occluding the wide array of styles and sensibilities found in the many anonymously designed pieces.[2] It has, moreover, encouraged a rather limited system of value judgements as to which sequences are worthy of our attention—one that I wish to challenge.

The most notable result of such an approach has been the obscuring of sequences made before 1954. This was the year that marked Bass's entry into the field with his title design for *Carmen Jones* (Otto Preminger). So often have ill-informed journalists promulgated the myth that only from this point forward did film titles begin to incorporate anything more ambitious than a couple of pleasing decorations that it has gained an unfortunate popular acceptance.[3] As we shall see, the history of film title sequences is far more complex and diverse than we are so often given to believe.

My purpose in writing this article is threefold. Firstly, I wish to illustrate some of the fantastic array of choices that filmmakers have made in order to get us excited about their upcoming films. Secondly, I endeavour to show some of the ways in which cultural, technological, and industrial factors have come together to shape the historically changing ways in which they have chosen to do so. Finally, through pursuing these ends, I hope to reinstate into popular acceptance the value and pleasures of just a few of the many thousands of forgotten and under-appreciated sequences from the first half of the twentieth century in particular. In so doing, I aim to foster a better understanding of how designers and directors have envisaged and sought to contribute to the ways in which we experience cinema.

Tracing a history of opening title sequences from the silent period through to the present day we are able to see how the stylistic norms of different cinematic eras have often followed distinct evolutionary lines. In particular, we can observe an increasingly manifest desire to use title sequences in order to do more than simply provide a list of credits. The different elements of the title sequences examined—image, sound, and lettering—all come together to shape our expectations of the film to come and often do so in ways that echo broader filmmaking tendencies and trends.

An overall pattern is distinct: one which leads towards longer, more complex sequences that increasingly resemble the style and content of the main part of the feature film but which also serve to present ever greater amounts of non-credit information in ways that are sometimes oblique.

Straightforward statistical analysis thus shows that stylistic norms have shifted through the years from dominantly plain backgrounds to the use of appropriate still pictures, thence to moving images, and, finally, to action sequences that contribute significantly to the film's backstory or to its main narrative drive. At the same time, a host of other smaller cycles and groupings can be discerned, which sometimes break away from the dominant trends. Some of these are short-lived historical cycles; others span wider periods of time and are associated instead with films that fit into particular cinematic groupings. In either case, the incidence of sets of title sequences with distinct collective features is invariably part and parcel of broader variations and changes within mainstream American cinema.

Before embarking upon a chronological survey of the history of American film title sequences, it seems important to emphasise that—irrespective of their degree of fit with wider groupings and trends—the majority of title sequences have been carefully tailored to fit the particular film that they introduce. Let us take, by way of example, *The Women* (George Cukor, 1939). Adapted from a popular stage play, this comedy drama featured a star-laden ensemble cast of deliciously bitchy characters. Its title sequence incorporated a series of vignettes of its principal players, each preceded by the image of an animal deemed emblematic of their character's disposition and whose facial shape or expression often resembled that of the actor. Indicating that the film had been cast to type, it thus compared Joan Crawford to a leopard, Joan Fontaine to a lamb, and Marjorie Main to a horse!

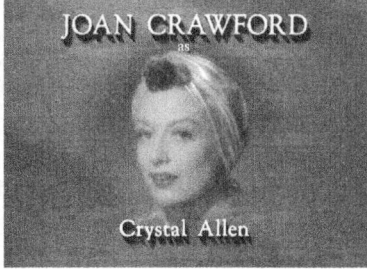

The Women (1939)

With this example in mind, it is perhaps also worth briefly expanding upon just a few of the ways in which individually tailored features have tended to exist within some kind of standardised framework. There is, in particular, a degree to which the title sequence for *The Women* typifies its period of production, as the 1930s was the era in which the presentation of a series of actor/character vignettes was at its popular height. Like most sequences of its time, it seeks to whet audience appetite for the coming film without direct recourse to narrative action. Structurally, the sequence stands alone: it does not advance the plot, it contains no dialogue or sound effects, and it fades to black before the main film begins. Where it does differ from conventions of the 1930s is in its length, being of far greater duration than any other example I have found from this era. The sequence also contains features characteristic of its genre: like most other comic films, its choice of image and music sets a light and humorous tone. Finally, embellished by images of its host of well-known players it illustrates—like *Grand Hotel* (Edmund Goulding, 1932)—the quality on which MGM most prided itself: that this was the product of a studio that boasted "more stars than there are in heaven".

Film genre and production studio have often been associated with particular stylistic features in film title sequences, just as they have in movies more broadly. It is, for instance, unlikely to come as a great surprise that film musicals have tended to feature songs during their opening titles more often than we find in other genres, with examples to be found in *Thin Ice* (Sidney Lanfield, 1937), *Babes on Broadway* (Busby Berkeley, 1941), and *Singin' in the Rain* (Gene Kelly and Stanley Donen, 1952). In an earlier article I have shown how title sequences in Westerns, such as *Stagecoach* (John Ford, 1939) and *Winchester '73* (Anthony Mann, 1950), have featured action and movement far more than have those of other genres.[4] We can see from these examples that generic norms operate in opening title sequences to rapidly introduce what are arguably the genres' primary pleasures.

The association that we sometimes find between title sequence features and their production studio is the product of a slightly different dynamic. Although such common features may sometimes contribute to the unique requirements of the film at hand, their main purpose is more often to promote the studio itself as a producer of calibre. The Warner Bros. studio, for instance, often chose to propel its logo into the limelight through its greater than average willingness to allow filmmakers to tamper with it. Variations and assaults upon their famous trademark can be found in films so diverse as *The Adventures of Robin Hood* (Michael Curtiz, 1938), where it is rendered in an elaborately illuminated style reminiscent of a medieval manuscript, *Robin and the Seven Hoods* (Gordon Douglas, 1964), in which it is riddled by machine gun pellets, *Blazing Saddles* (Mel Brooks, 1974), in which it is burned to cinders, and *Gremlins 2: The New Batch* (Joe Dante, 1990), where Bugs Bunny and Daffy Duck fight for possession of it.

The Adventures of Robin Hood (1938) and *Blazing Saddles* (1974)

Above all, though, many styles of titling are strongly associated with the era in which the film was produced. Through the decades, we are often able to observe a refining of process that tends be characterised in critical terms as 'development' or 'evolution': a pattern of change that is both linear and cumulative. As I have already suggested, as time went on title sequences became more and more likely to include live-action footage, sound effects, and dialogue: the same kinds of ingredients as the main part of the film.

Not all stylistic changes have been linear, however; sometimes relatively short-lived cycles have come and gone. This has normally come about when designers have copied the innovation of a celebrated title designer. Sequences designed by Saul Bass in the 1950s and 1960s, such as *The Man with the Golden Arm* (Otto Preminger, 1955) and *Spartacus* (Stanley Kubrick, 1960), and by Kyle Cooper in the 1990s, such as *Se7en* (David Fincher, 1995) and *The Island of Dr. Moreau* (John Frankenheimer, 1996), have given rise to waves of shameless imitators.

In other cases, fashions for a particular style have arisen because they have been deemed appropriate to a certain type of film that exists as a production cycle. For instance, title sequences for the sci-fi, horror, and exploitation films of the 1950s are often characterised by the melodramatic excesses of a crashing score and huge credit lettering. We can find examples in *When Worlds Collide* (Rudolph Maté, 1951), where roaring flames and explosions of fire wipe away the words of the main title; *It Came from Outer Space* (Jack Arnold, 1953), in which the main title is of enormous size and appears to project forward out of the screen thanks in part to the movie's 3D technique; and *Forbidden Planet* (Fred. M. Wilcox, 1956), which, in similar fashion, appears to project its letters forward from a central point in the lower background, capitalising, in this case, upon the dramatic potential of the CinemaScope image.

The history of film titling that I present here draws its

material from a sample of roughly 3,000 opening title sequences from American feature films of the sound period.[5] Although outside the scope of my main survey, I preface it with some material on silent movies compiled largely with the aid of secondary sources. While difficulties in accessing archive materials prevent me from doing justice to opening titles in silent cinema, I feel it is important to highlight some of their innovations.

I have organised my account chronologically, dividing it into six periods of unequal duration: silent cinema; sound cinema to 1939; 1940–54; 1955–74; 1975–94; and 1995 to the present day. The placement of these divisions is not without a degree of arbitrariness, I will admit, but it is also governed by my perception of a series of steps in the progression of title sequence design, according to one or both of two principles. The first is the relative conformity of key characteristics and the second is linearity of stylistic change.

Such groupings are naturally clumsy, since significant variations exist within each group while other characteristics bridge the end of one time period and the beginning of another. They are intended to help provide an overview and I have endeavoured to highlight variations and subgroups in my discussion. It is perhaps worth noting also that some of these divisions correspond to those made by other historians of American cinema. For instance they might be seen to roughly match or to further subdivide what Douglas Gomery has identified as the "four fundamental eras in the history of Hollywood as industry".[6] These are the rise of Hollywood from the late nineteenth century to the coming of sound, the studio era of the 1930s and 1940s, the television broadcasting age beginning with the rise of television in the 1950s, and the era inaugurated by the coming of the feature film blockbuster in the mid-1970s.[7]

AUSPICIOUS BEGINNINGS: CREDITS IN SILENT CINEMA

The very earliest films had no opening or closing credit sequences. The earliest 'author' credited in films appears to have been the production company. According to Earl Theisen, the first credit titles appeared in 1897 when Thomas Edison used a two-inch strip of film to display his name and copyright.[8] Other producers followed suit. Instead of placing the credit on a separate title card at the beginning or end of the film, however, many production companies of this era responded to widespread film piracy by incorporating their logos into the main body of the film. An international phenomenon, the technique was perhaps most famously deployed by the pioneering French director George Méliès, with his Star Films logo plainly visible on the sets of such films as *Les aventures de Robinson Crusoe* (1902) and *Les Royaume des fées* (1903).[9] Although it may strike today's audiences as a rather peculiar practice, the incorporation of such an overt mark of authorship and ownership would certainly have seemed less disruptive to viewers of early non-narrative films than to audiences of later years. Only once the 'cinema of attractions' gave way to a cinema of cogent narrative space and logic would such a mark have come to seem inappropriate. By the time this occurred, other important factors had already come into play.

Several elements combined to extend the number of credits presented and this escalation encouraged production companies to group them at the beginning and/or end of the film. The evolution of the star system was probably the most important, although the first documented credit to an individual was that of André Heuzé, a writer for the French Pathé Frères production company, in 1906.[10] The first actor to be credited in the United States is reported to be G. M. Anderson, star of a series of Broncho Billy Westerns from 1908. This prestige is doubtless linked to the fact that Anderson also wrote and produced the films and was part-owner of their production studio, Essanay.[11] In 1912, the writer's name began to appear in American film credits. Janet Staiger explains, "the industry argued that this practice encouraged submissions from famous writers and decreased possibilities of plagiarism".[12] Throughout the 1910s and 1920s, the number of credited personnel escalated rapidly as feature length narratives became a popular cinematic form and the evolving studio system ensured that the prestige of the personnel involved was maintained through recurrent associations with quality products for which they would be credited.

As opening titles and intertitles became increasingly significant features of silent films, their presentation came to be afforded greater importance. The first wave of stylistic flamboyance occurred in the late 1910s. David Bordwell claims that 'art titles' were common by the 1920s and cites *The Narrow Trail* (William S. Hart, 1917) as an early example. By 1923, he is able to locate an example of moving background images in *The Merry-Go-Round* (Rupert Julian and Erich von Stroheim, 1923) and, the following year, an instance of animation in the title sequence to *The Speed Spook* (Charles Hines, 1924).[13]

By 1928, Herbert McKay was one of several writers instructing amateur filmmakers in the mechanics of creating a large repertory of 'novelty' and 'trick' titles as a way of dressing up both intertitles and opening credits. Although he indicated that similar techniques might be used for either type of title, he expressed a belief that the more ostentatious decorations should be reserved for the opening titles where they would not prove a distraction from the unfolding narrative. Many of the titles he suggested combined a notion of topical propriety with a spectacular demonstration of the mechanical/magical trickery of the cinematic apparatus. For example,

> *The Metal Legion*: The screen is seen covered with black granules. These granules shift and pull together and soon the granular form is changed to a crystalline form, the structure being needle-like. These needles rise on end and march in martial ranks to a common heap, where they merge with the rest of the mass. Soon these masses take the form of letters and soon the letters are clear-cut and distinct.

> *The Volcano*: Smoke rolls up across the screen in dense clouds. Letters become faintly seen through the smoke. The smoke fades as the letters become more and more distinct and finally the letters are formed of curling, rolling clouds of smoke illuminated with weird light while the background is black.

> *The Sandstorm*: An Arab encampment is seen in the desert, a sandstorm comes up and whirling sand fills the air, this swirls about and finally dies down. The camp has disappeared, the sand has been ranged in dunes which form the letters of the words. This is a most mysterious effect and one which always excites admiration.[14]

McKay's manual testifies to the levels of production time and technical ingenuity that were applied to the manufacture of some titles in this period. This can be read as indicative of their perceived importance. In citing his advice, it is not my intention to suggest that such experimentation was in any way the norm for films titles of the late silent period. Across the years, the titles of amateur and independent short films have, like their main content, been characterised by innovation and formal experimentation more often than mainstream commercial product. What I wish to emphasise is that some level of innovation and diversity did exist in film titles of this period and that the application of ingenuity and skill to title design was not purely a post-*Carmen Jones* phenomenon.

THAT'S ENTERTAINMENT: SOUND CINEMA TO 1939

With the coming of sound, experimentation with the technological possibilities of cinema was almost immediately extended from image to soundtrack. *The Terror* (Roy del Ruth, 1928), usually regarded as the second all-talking picture, also became the first without a single title. Instead of a conventional title sequence, its credits were spoken aloud by the star, Conrad Nagel.[15] Spoken titles did not, of course, become the norm—although a handful of later examples can be found, and there are even some films with titles that are wholly or partly sung, such as the musicals *Sweet Rosie O'Grady* (Irving Cummings, 1943) and *Meet Me After the Show* (Richard Sale, 1951). Journalist Grady Johnson claims of spoken titles that "the industry abandoned that technique when it realised people seldom remember what they hear".[16]

The desire to move away from the aesthetic of title cards also led to the production of a couple of films that used only end credits. Barry Salt cites *The Bellamy Trial* (Montana Bell, 1929) as one such example.[17] Johnson suggests that the speedy termination of this experiment derived from the exhibitors' practice of omitting end credits in order to turn the performances around more quickly.[18]

Aside from the brief dalliance with spoken credits, title sequences of the early sound period had much in common with their immediate predecessors. In line with the currently popular stereotype applied to this era, most were relatively simple, tending to place their titles over a plain background or else over or beside one or more still pictures. As the decade progressed, pictures displaced the popularity of plain backgrounds. Many of them pointed to narrative or generic features through one or more relevant motifs. Early examples of this technique include *Half Shot at Sunrise* (Paul Sloane, 1930), which places its titles over the image of a First World War battlefield, thus using the sequence to help establish setting. In similar fashion, the titles for *Morocco* (Josef von

Morocco (1930)

Sternberg, 1930) appear over a scenic image that describes the film's locale in a broadly iconographic sense while at the same time illustrating an archway that appears several times during the course of the film and through which Amy Jolly (Marlene Dietrich) will make her final exit at its conclusion. *Dracula* (Todd Browning, 1931) finds a slightly different motivation for the image it uses: a gleaming-eyed bat lurking behind a spider's web points up the film's generic credentials. Irrespective of visual style, opening title sequences of the 1930s were almost invariably accompanied by instrumental music. And yet, despite a general preference for simplicity, we continue to find a significant amount of novelty work; as attempts to dispense with opening titles waned, visual innovations continued and these sequences invariably remain a pleasure to watch.

Grady Johnson lists a plethora of effects used during this period:

> The name of the picture appeared in flaming letters, in floating lilies on a pond [...], carved in wax and melted, machine-gunned into the side of a building, coiled in rope or twined in growing vines, on plate glass windows that were broken, or in the dirt spray of skidding automobiles.[19]

As these examples signal, the novelty sequences of the 1930s often centred upon the inscription of main titles onto physical objects, or else the utilisation of objects in such a way as to reveal or destroy those titles. Amongst the films that display the act or revealing or erasing titles are *Her Man* (Tay Garnett, 1930), where waves wash away titles scraped into the sand; *The Mummy* (Karl Freund, 1932), where a revolving set reveals the main title on the side of a model pyramid; and *Maytime* (Robert Z.

Maytime (1937)

Leonard, 1937), where some of the credits are carved into a tree trunk and others appear as blossom floating on a stream. It was to such sequences as these that Saul Bass paid tribute in his own opening credit sequence for *That's Entertainment, Part II* (Gene Kelly, 1976), a fact that acquires considerable irony when one considers how often the widespread celebration of his other works has been used to justify the dismissal of the sequences of the thirties and forties.[20]

Such novelty designs normally drew their inspiration from the film's subject matter or location. This was also true of most films that used still pictures to illustrate their titles. Some title designs were based on other criteria, however. During this period, several of the major production companies developed house styles for their title sequences. These highlighted studio authorship and, in this sense, adopted a similar role to the logos that normally preceded them. They emphasised consistency rather than difference and, in so doing, displaced the more usual primary function of introducing salient features of the individual picture (although star credits maintained this role to some degree). The relationships between house styles, production company logos, and the films introduced varied from studio to studio. For instance, between 1933 and 1935, Twentieth Century Fox often employed a style that referenced neither their logo nor the individual films. It involved an unusual lettering style which was, like the background, filled with a distinctive abstract pattern. It can be seen in *Advice to the Lovelorn* (Alfred Werker, 1933), *Bulldog Drummond Strikes Back* (Roy del Ruth, 1934), and *Les Misérables* (Richard Boleslawski, 1935) amongst others. By contrast, a style used by MGM between 1938 and 1940 made specific reference to the famous studio logo through its use of a lion's profile as a title background. Examples can be seen in *A Christmas Carol* (Edwin L. Marin, 1938), *Ninotchka* (Ernst Lubitsch, 1939), and *Comrade X* (King Vidor, 1940).

The most well-remembered house style is almost certainly one used by Warner Bros. as a regular feature from 1932 to 1935 and occasionally thereafter. Looking back, it seems emblematic of not only the output of the Warner studio but a whole period of filmmaking. These title sequences centred on a series of brief portrait shots of the cast, with both actor and character names superimposed. Split-screens were often used for the lesser players and the shots were separated by wipes. This appears to be the only style introduced during the 1930s that relied on technological development. Barry Salt reports that the optical printers needed to produce this effect were available for studios to purchase from 1930 and a regular use of wipes had been established by 1932. Warners, he notes, used significantly more wipes than any other studio.[21] We can therefore think of title sequences such as *Three on a Match* (Mervyn Le Roy, 1932), *The Mayor of Hell* (Archie Mayo, 1933), and *Fashions of 1934* (William Dieterle, 1934) as being consistent with the broader studio style. At the same time, using footage of the cast pointed to features of the individual films introduced.

Irrespective of their content and design, almost all title sequences of the 1930s were autonomous, free-standing segments that were clearly separate from the subsequent footage, in terms of both sound and image. Even where motion photography was used, as in *Cavalcade* (Frank Lloyd, 1933), with its horseback riders, or *Condemned Women* (Lew Landers, 1938), which centres its title sequence around prison scenes, the material almost never participated in the chain of narrative events that began to unfold after the titles ended. Pre-title sequences were virtually unknown in these years, although *20,000 Years in Sing Sing* (Michael Curtiz, 1933) provides one noteworthy exception. Yet rather than using its pre-title sequence to begin the narrative action, as later films would do, it used it to explain the etymology of the main title and to give it impact: 20,000 is the sum total of the

20,000 Years in Sing Sing (1933)

sentences allotted each of the inmates seen silhouetted during an impressively mounted opening montage.

A further feature that 1930s title sequences shared was their brevity. On average, they lasted for just 56 seconds, with *The Women* representing the only sequence in my sample that exceeded two minutes in length. Even that film's two-minutes-and-56-seconds sequence is just a fraction of the length of those found in later years when films such as *Martin* (George A. Romero, 1978), *Kansas City* (Robert Altman, 1995), and *Jerry Maguire* (Cameron Crowe, 1996) would have title sequences more than nine minutes long. The concision achieved by title sequences of the 1930s owed a great deal to the routine clustering of many credits onto each title card. This practice can be observed in such pictures as *Susan Lenox: Her Fall and Rise* (Robert Z. Leonard, 1931) and *Ladies in Love* (Edward H. Griffith, 1936). As we shall see, once this practice gave way to a spreading out of credits that caused titles sequences to run for longer, the implications for their design were considerable.

PICTURE PERFECT: 1940–1954

These years showed both continuity and change from the previous decade. Still pictures remained the most popular type of background image, increasing their dominance as some previously competing styles fell out of fashion. Plain backgrounds were used less and less, as filmmakers became ever keener to use the films' opening moments to introduce significant themes or motifs. At the same time, the more ostentatious titling styles lost their popularity. By the late 1930s, some low-budget features had reportedly spent up to one third of their production costs on the opening title sequence.[22] Gladwin Hill cites the reputed amount of $10,000 spent upon the enormous electric sign that forms the main title of *The Great Ziegfeld* (Robert Z. Leonard, 1936)—a far princelier sum at the time than it currently represents.[23]

For obvious reasons, such expenditure came to be thought of as inappropriate. Moreover, elaborate titling styles were often very much at odds with the aesthetics of the films they introduced. The 1940s and early 1950s are significant as the period in which many functions of title sequences that we now think of as standard were most effectively integrated with the narrational economy that characterises a high proportion of studio era films. That is, by advertising some of the films' main pleasures, they encouraged the audience to develop precisely the kinds of expectations that the individual films were designed to satisfy. Indeed, in forging ever closer links between the title sequence and what came after, these years would see the beginnings of a rapidly escalating trend in which many title sequences ceased to be structurally self-contained and began to extend the titles into the main narrative action.

Through the 1940s and early 1950s the average length of title sequences rose significantly. This can largely be accounted for by the spacing out of credits, so that key personnel such as the director and producer were increasingly allotted title cards of their own. This change was precipitated by the growing strength of unions, such as the writers' and directors' guilds, which successfully negotiated more prominent credit positioning for their members. Their demands included specifications about lettering size, on-screen duration, the acceptability or otherwise of sharing a card with other credits, and the order in which credits must appear. Although some credits continued to be negotiated individually and were enshrined in a filmmaker's own contract, in most cases they were the product of collective bargaining.

Agreements between major production companies and unions tended to be renegotiated every three years. This allowed for some changes in credit rules to occur, although most of the conventions with which we are now familiar were firmly in place by the early 1940s. The only significant disruption to the rights for which the unions pushed came in the 1950s as the HUAC investigations focused upon the film industry, at which time the blacklisting of hostile witnesses and the omission of their credits became common practice. One victim was the actor Howard Da Silva, whose credit was removed from *Slaughter Trail* (Irving Allen, 1951).[24] The Screen Writers Guild blacklisted some of its own members, refusing to extend to them the rights for which the union had fought so hard. *Friendly Persuasion* (William Wyler, 1956) has no screenplay credit at all, a fact that has been attributed to the blacklisting of writer Michael Wilson.[25] A host of other 1950s films, such as *The Defiant Ones* (Stanley Kramer, 1958), resorted to the use of pseudonymous names.[26]

The increasing length of title sequences had substantial implications for their visual design. With hindsight, some of the ways in which designers responded seem almost inevitable, and yet other choices are more surprising. The most obvious effect of spreading out the credits whilst not, at this stage, significantly increasing their numbers, was to make visible a great deal more of the background space. This, in turn, encouraged creative use of this space and, during this period, we find the regularity with which plain backgrounds were used sank to less than half that of the 1930s.

In the early 1940s, almost two thirds of title sequences used still images of some kind, during what would be this style's most popular period ever. Many such sequences employed just a single image. These were often motifs specific to the narrative, such as the eponymous bird in *The Maltese Falcon* (John Huston, 1941). Others made use of elaborate series of images, which often described characters or narrative situations, as is the case with the cartoons of *Presenting Lily Mars* (Norman Taurog, 1943) and *Grounds for Marriage* (Robert Z. Leonard, 1950). Others yet employed generic imagery so that, for instance, images of dancers opened the musicals *Song of the Islands* (Walter Lang, 1942) and *Dancing in the Dark* (Irving Reis, 1949). Yet, despite such efforts to find appropriate imagery with which to open films of the 1940s and early 1950s, there is little evidence of willingness to spend the kind of money on title sequences that we sometimes observed in earlier years.

One possible reason why inexpensiveness and relative simplicity were preferred at this time—in contrast to the novelty work of the 1930s or the styles that would emerge from the mid-1950s onwards—is the reportedly popular practice of projecting the opening titles onto closed theatre curtains.[27] Whether this was a cause or effect remains questionable, however. Yet another explanation suggests itself for the relative visual simplicity and lack of technological sophistication that characterised the majority of Hollywood film titles at this time. We may hypothesise that it was born at least in part of a movement towards a style that many writers have seen as characteristic of the 'classical' era; that is, the avoidance of drawing attention to any technical artifice that was not in itself a marketable commodity. And yet, while this interpretation doubtless has some merit, it is hard to regard it as fully satisfactory since it suggests a more substantial change in artistic vision between 1930s and 1940s Hollywood than there is evidence to support. Perhaps the only true answer lies in David Bordwell and Janet Staiger's observation that "the classical style has not changed in a cumulative or additive fashion".[28]

While still pictures continued to prevail during this period, a significant minority of films were beginning to explore techniques that have come to dominate title design to the present day. By incorporating diegetic moving images and, occasionally, diegetic sound, these sequences forge closer narrative and stylistic links with the main part of the film. In introducing narrative elements from the very first, they also served to launch the action with a greater immediacy than other types of opener. It was a trend that would take a firm hold within a relatively short period of time. In the early 1940s, just ten per cent of title sequences incorporated some degree of narrative action. Ten years later this figure had almost trebled, and so on until the early nineties saw two thirds of films using this technique. The use of pre-title sequences, which normally presented a short episode of action before the titles began, also grew significantly during this period. Examples include *Fixed Bayonets* (Samuel Fuller, 1951) and *The Glory Brigade* (Robert D. Webb, 1953), which both preface their title sequences with dramatic incidents. Such changes provide further indications of a growing desire on the part of filmmakers to introduce narrative elements from the film's very outset.

Although the popularity of action-based title sequences grew rapidly during these years, the move to incorporate diegetic sound happened more slowly. One of the first title sequences to combine diegetic sound with narrative action was *Destry Rides Again* (George Marshall, 1939), which depicted a tumult of unchecked lawlessness in a small Western town. Most films, though, continued to limit the acoustic accompaniment to non-diegetic music, and the use of dialogue was virtually unknown in title sequences of this era. A very rare instance can be found in *Kiss Tomorrow Goodbye* (Gordon Douglas, 1950), where titles unfurl over images of a busy law court. We see and hear the judge entering and banging his gavel to herald the title, 'Cagney Productions'. A voice announces that the court is in session. The gavel bangs again for the final director credit, after which the hearing proceeds. Even here the use of speech is very minimal. The fact that it was not widely adopted until much later can probably be attributed to a reluctance to place spoken and written words in competition with one another. Even in the contemporary cinema, where titles are commonly situated alongside action and dialogue, many sequences are designed to avoid presenting titles and important dialogue simultaneously.

In the range of title sequences made in the 1940s and early 1950s, we can see that changes in the dominant styles took some surprising turns. While most sequences had a much slicker look than those of the 1930s, they displayed less technical ingenuity. At the same time, a narrational and stylistic direction barely hinted at in the 1930s emerged as a dominant trend that would escalate in later years. The desegregation of sound and image, style and action, between the title sequence and the main part of the film is a dominant feature of American filmmaking from the 1960s onwards. In this earlier period, there exist discernible movements towards such unification, haphazard though they be. Title sequences entailing some level of narrative action, such as *Meet John Doe* (Frank Capra, 1941), *I Walked with a Zombie* (Jacques Tourneur, 1943), and *Miracle on 34th Street* (George Seaton, 1947) predate countless other less progressive sequences. Indeed, whilst the beginning of an undeniable trend is clear, there is no evidence of clear consensus on the part of the filmmaking community. The late 1950s and 1960s would in fact give rise to even greater stylistic diversification.

BASS, BOND, AND BEYOND: 1955–1974

Alongside auteurist prejudices, perhaps the main reason why film and design history has tended to overlook opening title sequences of the 1940s and early 1950s is that the key trend of this era was towards a relatively subtle, self-effacing sensibility. In developing their potential as a tool with which to guide audience expectations of the experience to come, many had taken on forms that were so closely entwined with the main part of the feature that they lend themselves poorly to being enjoyed without it. It is not entirely surprising, therefore, that these sequences are seldom selected to be shown as clips in lectures on titling history, or uploaded onto internet pages of 'great' title sequences. Yet this attitude does them grave disservice. For film scholars seeking to understand American cinema's aesthetic history, moreover, the trends and cycles of titling style can often prove useful indices of the tides, waves, and undercurrents of wider cinematic changes.

Title sequences of the mid-1950s to mid-1970s, and especially this period's first ten years, have attracted far more critical interest than earlier ones, but the styles for which this era is most famous—abstract animation and other aesthetics drawn from outside the domain of mainstream cinema—are actually representative of just a small minority of films. Richard Avedon's striking collage for *Funny Face* (Stanley Donen, 1957), the elegant simplicity of Wayne Fitzgerald's slow-motion shower of diamonds in *Imitation of Life* (Douglas Sirk, 1959), James Pollack's off-kilter animation for *The Birds* (Alfred Hitchcock 1963) and, in the UK, the designs of Maurice Binder and Robert Brownjohn for the James Bond movies provide just a handful of the most acclaimed examples of such technique. These designers' attention-grabbing sequences captured the interest of critics and filmmakers alike and many examples of their work are still renowned today. Yet the amount of attention such designs have received occludes the fact that the emergence of this trend was far less statistically significant than other developments. In other words, the cycle encompassed only a small proportion of films and lasted for a relatively short period of time.

Meanwhile, a fantastic array of other stylistic developments arose from a host of more pervasive changes in popular American filmmaking. These changes ranged from the breakdown of the studio system and the 'classical' style to the burgeoning popularity of widescreen cinema and to the increasing synergy between the film and music businesses and consequent rise of the pop music soundtrack. While overtly authored experimental animations most certainly deserve to be celebrated, ignorance of the other trends perpetuates a false and impoverished understanding of the range of ways in which filmmakers responded to the new technical, industrial, and cultural challenges of the era.

The most common titling styles throughout this period furthered the dominant trends that had emerged during the previous fifteen or twenty years. Title sequences continued to get longer, reaching an average length of almost two-and-a-half minutes by the early 1970s. A growing proportion centred on narrative action, and many incorporated diegetic sound effects and, later, dialogue. The use of pre-title sequences also increased, as did their average length.

In title sequences of this period we can therefore detect two contrasting impulses. On the one hand we can observe the growing dominance of title sequences that move to integrate themselves, as far as possible, with the main body of the film. By such means, these sequences meet their obligation to credit cast and crew but, at the same time, they divert attention away from the act of direct address that the credit lettering represents. On the other hand there is strong evidence of an increasing attraction to experimentation and innovation, a sensibility which may also be thought of as being of great importance to this era of American cinema more broadly. Sequences of this school flaunt their technique. In doing so, they draw attention to an activity that is at the core of what title sequences do: directly addressing the audience. It is hard to watch a sequence such as Elinor Bunin's stylish opener for the asylum-set melodrama *Lilith* (Robert Rossen, 1964)—in which soft and hazy images of fragile butterflies become entrapped by harsh black bars that multiply to form a spider's web—without reflecting upon the ways it courts one's complicity in preparing for the ensuing viewing experience.

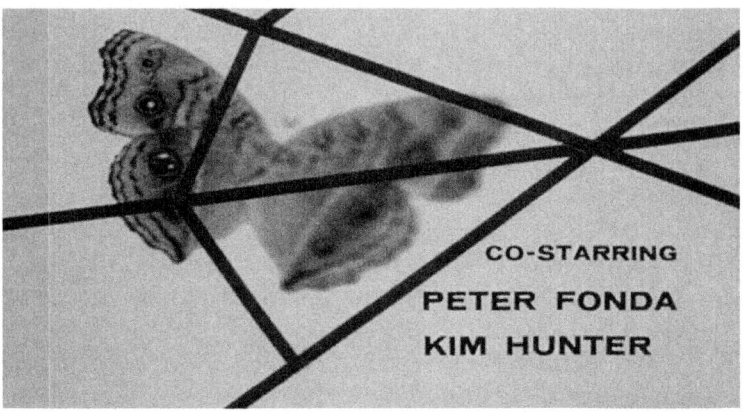

Lilith (1964)

Common to each of these schools of design we can also see the emergence of a number of subordinate trends, such as the growing use of theme songs and the movement towards asymmetrical placement of the credit titles. Sometimes attributable to industrial or technological causes, at other times these cycles and trends result from the widespread copying of critically and/or commercially successful formats.

Of the new cycle of stylistically flamboyant title sequences the most widely documented have been those designed by Saul Bass. If I have often taken issue with errors and elisions in the critical history of title sequences, here I must bow to convention in recognising the pioneering nature of his series of collaborations with the director Otto Preminger. Through these sequences we can observe many of the ways in which styles drawn from other media began to exert substantial influence on titling aesthetics. The arenas of advertising and graphic design—which occupied his professional background—can be seen as especially important in this respect, but links to avant-garde cinema also emerge.

Bass's work was so highly regarded that many contemporary designers sought to emulate his style. Others drew from his work an inspiration to experiment, even though their own styles and techniques were not in themselves derivative. Observant of the critical plaudits that such sequences often drew, directors and producers became increasingly keen to afford their designers the opportunity to make such explorations. As a result, there occurred a fashion for self-consciously flashy titling work for which the designers themselves were often credited on screen. This is the first time that we can unequivocally trace a titling design trend to an individual.

Saul Bass has invariably been the main focus of attention in histories of film titling, yet the encouragement offered by Preminger should not be undervalued. The director's existing enthusiasm for creating interesting titles using unconventional techniques is plainly evident in such earlier features as *Whirlpool* (1950) and *Where the Sidewalk Ends* (1950). The sensibility, if not the style, of Bass's early title designs for Preminger is not without context or precedent therefore. Indeed their partnership provides a fine example of the way in which fortuitous collaboration so often gives rise to ideas and products that seem to far exceed the sum of the collaborators' individual input. Unlike earlier, almost invariably anonymous, title designers however, Bass received on-screen credit from the start and his reputation was elevated by increasingly widespread recognition of distinct and consistent authorial traits. This is not to say that all his work looked superficially similar—although in the late 1950s he was particularly fond of animating silhouettes cut from paper as in *The Man with the Golden Arm* (Otto Preminger, 1955) and *Anatomy of a Murder* (Otto Preminger, 1959)—but rather that his diverse techniques emerged from a clearly formulated conception of the ideal purpose of title sequences: in his own words, to "symbolise and summarise" the film.[29] Whether he used animation, live action, special effects, or a mixture of all three—as in *The Big Knife* (Robert Aldrich, 1955), *Vertigo* (Alfred Hitchcock, 1958), and *North by Northwest* (Alfred Hitchcock, 1959)—each sequence was designed around one or more important motifs bearing strong thematic links to the film being introduced. Each sequence differed in style from the main part of the film, standing alone in a structural sense. It is a quality that has lent them well to display outside their original context—in lectures, museum exhibitions, gallery installations, and so forth—thereby reinforcing Bass's reputation even while some of the films his work supported have quietly slipped into obscurity.

While Bass placed a central importance upon the search for a key image representative of each film, many of his contemporary imitators were less concerned with such a quest than with the inspiration they drew from his visual stylishness and use of mixed media. Bass himself was very dismissive of such projects:

> Producers, film-makers and title-makers began to regard the titles as a personal tap-dance that they did before the film began. All sorts of showing off went on [...]. I find it disturbing to see titles that I regard as fashionable, idiosyncratic performances of novelty for novelty's sake. We saw a lot of pyro-technics and fun and games that didn't necessarily support the film.[30]

It is ironic that what we might call the 'YouTube effect' has all but eliminated the original context and purpose of individual title sequences, placing value on the very qualities that Bass so roundly criticises.

The creation of titles that upstage the film—ironically, Bass's own sequence for *Walk on the Wild Side* (Edward Dmytryk, 1962) is often heralded as a classic example—has normally been regarded as a cardinal sin. Nevertheless, the string of flashily 'authored' title sequences that were emerging by the early 1960s are of profound historical interest, variable though their success as film introductions may have been.

The interest lies in their exemplification of an aesthetic that was shortly to become a characteristic of many American films of the 1960s. Richard Corliss notes that designers such as Saul Bass, Wayne Fitzgerald, and Maurice Binder were using "all the resources of cinema in their three-minute 'films': animation, live-actions, split-screens, strobe and slow-motion photography, still photos and drawings, archive material, any and all combinations of the above".[31] Techniques used frequently by experimental filmmakers of the period, but which were seldom features of mainstream cinema, were now drawn into commercial films by means of the title sequence. Maurice Binder's abstract designs for *Charade* (Stanley Donen, 1963) and *Arabesque* (Stanley Donen, 1966), Pablo Ferro's daring split-screens for *The Thomas Crown Affair* (Norman Jewison, 1968), and Don Record's pop art montage for *How Sweet It Is!* (Jerry Paris, 1968) are just a few examples. This forum for the wide dissemination of abstract and avant-garde cinema allowed significant additions to be made to the repertoire of mainstream filmmaking even if, as Bass suggests, such sequences did not always sit well with the films they were intended to support.

How Sweet It Is! (1968)

By the late 1960s and early 1970s, another notable, if not especially prevalent, design practice had emerged. An increasing use of parody and pastiche signalled an increasingly widespread project of examining and re-working the heritage of title design. These techniques were used to various ends. Irreverent parodies often achieved comic effect, as in Wayne Fitzgerald's design for *Cat Ballou* (Elliot Silverstein, 1965), where the Columbia logo's demure Lady Liberty stripped off her toga to reveal the costume of a gun-toting cowgirl. Many films pastiched the styles of previous years to signal a period setting: *The Sting* (George Roy Hill, 1973), for instance, used the whole gamut of old-style features, ranging from an obsolete version of the studio logo to the placement of credits on turning book pages—a style that had all but disappeared after the 1940s ended. Foregrounding and reworking classic features of title design style signalled a growing self-awareness in the field. This can be seen as emblematic of American film-makers' increasingly wider knowledge of, and reference to, the heritage from which their work emerged.

As I indicated earlier, although self-consciousness and ostentation are more strongly associated with the 1950s and 1960s than they are with other eras of title design, they did not dominate the field at this time, when the strongest design trend was the increased reliance on narrative action. During these years, other features emerged that had no strong alignment to any school of visual design. For one thing, the use of title songs more than doubled from twelve per cent in the early 1950s to thirty per cent by the late 1960s. As I have argued in some detail elsewhere, their increased popularity appears to owe much to the Oscar success of the theme to *High Noon* (Fred Zinnemann, 1952), within the Western genre at least, and to the growing realisation of the benefits of cross-promoting music and film more generally.[32]

A visual innovation was the move towards asymmetrically positioned titles. Broader industrial reasons would seem to lie at the root of this trend too, as they emerged shortly after the American film industry moved to adopt widescreen formats. Indeed, most of the earliest uses of decentralised titles can be found in widescreen films, such as *Written on the Wind* (Douglas Sirk, 1956) and *I Married a Woman* (Hal Kanter, 1956). It therefore appears

that designers embraced them in direct response to the
need to find new frame compositions that would suit the
wider image formats.

The general pattern of change that we see between
the late 1950s and early 1970s, then, is a splitting-off in
two main directions. The most statistically significant
followed on from earlier years. This was the trend toward
the narrative and stylistic integration of title sequences
with the main part of the film. The most critically noted, on
the other hand, was a reversion to free-standing credits,
stylistically flashy and, unlike the novelty work of the
1930s, overtly authored. Some titles sequences, such as
the one designed by Don Record for *Prime Cut* (Michael
Ritchie, 1972), skilfully melded both trends; here, a lengthy
action sequence plays a crucial role in launching the plot,
yet it is filmed in a far more stylised way than the main
part of the feature, while its subtle yet effective animation
of the credit lettering is both stylish and witty.

The cultural, technological, and industrial factors that
give rise to such a complex nexus of stylistic directions in
film titling worked similarly upon the American cinema
more broadly in an era that is often thought of as one of
particular upheaval and reinvention. The history of title
design in this period can thus be regarded as not just a
lot more complex than is normally acknowledged but also
as an effective case study of the mechanisms underlying
aesthetic changes that would prove to be of both short
and long-term significance.

BEGINNINGS AND ENDINGS: 1975–1994

This was an era in which long strides were taken in
redressing what had widely come to be seen as the
excesses of earlier years, with filmmakers for the most
part eschewing excessively long or complex opening title

sequences. Yet, as so often before, many of the most notable stylistic changes were rooted in technical and industrial factors.

We have already seen how changes to credit rules through the late 1930s and 1940s gave rise to longer opening title sequences, which encouraged, in turn, some more inspired usage of the time during which these titles unfurled. Toward the latter part of the 1970s, by which point legal stipulations obliged filmmakers to include an ever-increasing number of names, the opening credit roll was starting to become quite untenable. Facing a backlash against seemingly interminable opening titles, repositioning the majority or credits to the end of the film must have seemed like an ideal solution. This time around, contractual obligations would discourage exhibitors from cutting them off as they had reportedly done in the 1920s.[33]

The result of this shift was a temporary fall in the average length of opening titles which, unsurprisingly, had a significant knock-on effect upon their design. Just as had been the case with short title sequences in the past, narrative material was included less often and, concomitantly, many sequences also reverted to a stand-alone format.

Plain black backgrounds enjoyed a new-found popularity, often in conjunction with striking computer-animation of the main title itself. This was a feature that reflected both the strengthening sway of new computer technologies and their graphic capabilities—with early and influential examples to be found in *Superman* (Richard Donner, 1978) and *Alien* (Ridley Scott, 1979)—and the increasing importance of instantly recognisable logos as cross-promotional merchandising became ever more heavily relied upon to increase the revenue streams associated with blockbuster and family movies in an age of huge entertainment conglomerates.

Ghostbusters II (Ivan Reitman, 1989) is one film which has no written titles at all at its beginning. The logo from the first film, animated so that the ghost holds up two fingers to represent sequel status, acts as the main title in conjunction with the hit-record theme song. Yet if *Ghostbusters II* successfully establishes an appropriately comedic, feel-good tone while referencing an established narrative and generic template, what many other such sequences arguably did less well than their predecessors was to subtly nudge audiences into the psychological space where they would be most positively receptive to the film ahead.

From the late 1980s onwards, a slightly different pattern starts to emerge, however. Again, we can understand this in relation to the shifting structures of the American film industry. The erosion of the studio system as a vertically integrated oligopoly had given rise to increasingly complex film financing arrangements which, through the eighties and beyond, would involve the participation of multiple organisations in the production and distribution of most films. The names and logos of these companies could not be tucked away at the end of the picture as so many individual credits had been but would instead be placed at the very, very start of the film. Yet rather than placing all opening credits alongside this group, many filmmakers of the period would opt to insert an often-lengthy narrative sequence between this and another later credits cluster. *The Running Man* (Paul Michael Glaser, 1987), *King of New York* (Abel Ferrara, 1990), and *The Getaway* (Roger Donaldson, 1994) all offer good examples of this technique. Such action interims between the two credit groups served to maintain the earlier popular tradition of using a pre-title sequence to launch the narrative as quickly as possible. In this respect, little had changed from earlier years except that a group of titles preceded the pre-title sequence (which might now perhaps be better dubbed a 'mid-title sequence') as well as following it.

Critical consensus seems to be that the 1980s and early 1990s contributed relatively few notable innovations in the history of film titling. Undoubtedly the most important, however, were the fledgling moves towards the computer generated motion graphics that would be more rigorously exploited in the years that followed and, in particular, those films such as *Superman* which made the moving letter forms a central part of the sequence's visual design. Less significant from a teleological point of view, but often intriguing and at times highly entertaining, was the trend toward parody and pastiche which had begun to emerge in the late 1960s and early 1970s and which would become increasingly widespread. In particular, alteration and incorporation of production company logos was rife. Examples include *Tarzan the Ape Man* (John Derek, 1981), in which the MGM lion utters the hero's trademark cry instead of his customary roar, as well as *Strange Brew* (Dave Thomas, 1983), *Indiana Jones and the Temple of Doom* (Steven Spielberg, 1984), *Coming to America* (John Landis, 1988), *The Burbs* (Joe Dante, 1988), *Scrooged* (Richard Donner, 1988), and *Edward Scissorhands* (Tim Burton, 1990).

Despite a continued smattering of interesting and innovative sequences that served their movies well, the relative insipidity of titling norms during this period might lead us to the conclusion that film titles are at their most provocative when the dominant cinema is in a state of flux caused by new technologies, industrial changes, or influences from other national cinemas. Indeed, a couple of the design features that did emerge can be attributed to those very factors: the bipartite clustering of titles came in response to industry restructuring whilst the animation of letterforms was closely linked to the increasing sophistication of computer graphics. In the years that followed, title design responded to the growing exploitation of computer capabilities across a range of visual media and by the mid-1990s a new wave of interest in title design was in full flow.

THE SHAPE OF THINGS TO COME: 1995–PRESENT DAY

The current revival of critical interest in title sequences began to gather speed during the early 1990s. Once again, Saul Bass was at the vanguard when, after a long hiatus, he was lured back into title design work. Most notably, he and his wife Elaine created four celebrated sequences for director Martin Scorsese. These were *Goodfellas* (1990), *Cape Fear* (1991), *The Age of Innocence* (1993), and *Casino* (1995), which was Bass's final sequence before his death in 1996.

The sequence that really got people talking, though, was made by a relative newcomer. This was Kyle Cooper's design for *Se7en*. The popularity of this particular sequence hinged upon its use of 'MTV' aesthetics, the origins of which lie much further back in the structural/materialist

Se7en (1995)

work of American avant-garde directors such as Owen Land. Its style spawned a host of imitators, both in film titling and in other fields of graphic design. In particular, the scratchy, jumpy typography it used became almost ubiquitous for several years afterwards. Indeed, the sequence rapidly acquired a significance that extended beyond film titling, and even the film industry at large. This was acknowledged by the *New York Times Magazine*, which lauded the sequence as one of the most important design innovations of the decade.[34]

Cooper was just one of several title designers to develop a profile in the 1990s. The continued work of older designers such as Wayne Fitzgerald, Pablo Ferro, and Dan Perri was supplemented by striking work from Robert Dawson, Nina Saxon, Deborah Ross, Randy Balsmeyer, and Mimi Everett, to name but a few. Yet while the cult of individual creativity still holds sway when discussing film titles, especially in popular film journalism, other factors have become increasingly significant in shaping the titling aesthetics of the late 1990s and early twenty-first century.

One is the multiple fields of design in which many of these workers are employed. For instance, Daniel Kleinman, who has directed the title sequences to the James Bond films from *GoldenEye* (Martin Campbell, 1995) onwards, had previously worked in the music video industry. This background is very evident in his titling work, perhaps never more than in his sequence for *Tomorrow Never Dies* (Roger Spottiswoode, 1997). Kyle Cooper has directed commercial campaigns for several prominent companies including AT&T and Reebok.[35] Imaginary Forces, the company that he co-founded in 1996, has also worked extensively in interactive design. Such a cross-fertilisation of styles and ideas between these various design fields has undoubtedly contributed to the high degree of experimentation that can be observed in contemporary title design.

The increasing sophistication of computer software has encouraged and facilitated stylistic experimentation, permitting the creation of effects that would not have been achievable previously. The manipulation of typography has, as previously noted, proved especially appealing to designers in these years, with examples to be seen in *Sphere* (Barry Levinson, 1998), *The Avengers* (Jeremiah Chechik, 1998), and *Hollow Man* (Paul Verhoeven, 2000). In each of these sequences, the lettering is designed to participate in the theme of the film. For example, *Hollow Man*—an update of H. G. Wells' *The Invisible Man* that addresses the scientific manipulation of the body's makeup—animates its title lettering to resemble cells floating around in the blood stream, while the choice of translucent letters partakes of the invisibility motif.

New technologies have also meant that exciting sequences can be produced more cheaply than before. Using sophisticated but relatively inexpensive computer software, some companies have chosen to specialise in low-budget design bringing striking opening titles within the price range of any independent filmmaker. Courtesy of Bureau, for instance, the relatively small-scale *Safe* (Todd Haynes, 1995) has been provided with an opener every bit as effective as Bureau's design for the considerably more commercial *American Psycho* (Mary Harron, 2000).

At the opposite end of the scale, the re-emergence of an attitude that regards title sequences as interesting and enjoyable viewing material in their own right has led to the replication of a situation seen back in the 1930s. This is the investment of vast amounts of time and money in title sequences, the main purpose of which seems to be to showcase innovation and skill. One of the most notable is *Fight Club* (David Fincher, 1999). Its title sequence, showing an anatomically accurate journey through the human brain, reportedly took a team of designers the best part of two years to create.[36]

The newest wave that we are seeing now, however, is films that have virtually dispensed with the opening title sequence. This strategy goes much further than earlier movements to deflect attention from the credit titles by placing them over action scenes. Moreover, this development has occurred very rapidly and has become extremely widespread in a short space of time. Since 2000, forty per cent of the films I have surveyed have opening title sequences of less than thirty seconds in length. This compares with thirteen per cent in the late 1990s, and never more than seven per cent in any five-year period before that. Although films have occasionally done this before—*Around the World in 80 Days* (Michael Anderson, 1956) lacked even a main title, and is famous for having an unusually lengthy animated end credit sequence designed by Saul Bass—only recently has it begun to happen regularly.

In many ways this is not a surprising development. Throughout cinema's history, periods of intense experimentation and flamboyance in title design have invariably been followed by a backlash in which relative simplicity was favoured for a while. Yet far from heralding the death of the title sequence, the growing interest in film titles shown by today's design students suggests that, far from becoming a thing of the past, we can look forward to seeing a great deal more creativity in the future. In the meantime, with films like *Watchmen* (Zack Snyder, 2009) continuing to thrust original and eye-popping titles onto our screens, we have no legitimate reason to press fast-forward.

NOTES

1. Herbert C. McKay, *Amateur Movie Making* (New York: Falk Publishing, 1928), 165.
2. One notable exception is Gemma Solana and Antonio Boneu's recent book, *Uncredited: Graphic Design and Opening Titles in Movies* (Barcelona: Index Book, 2007).
3. Dick Blackburn, "Opening Flourish", *Guardian* (London): *The Guide*, 17 February 1996, 4; David Thomson, "The Man with the Golden Pen", *Independent on Sunday* (London), 21 June 1998, 19.
4. Deborah Allison, "Title Sequences in the Western Genre: The Iconography of Action", *Quarterly Review of Film and Video*, vol. 25, no. 2 (2008), 107–15.
5. Discussion of the sampling and statistical methods used can be found in my doctoral thesis, which was based upon a slightly smaller survey of 2,636 title sequences. Deborah Allison, *Promises in the Dark: Opening Title Sequences in American Feature Films of the Sound Period*, (PhD diss., University of East Anglia, 2001), 22–28.
6. Douglas Gomery, "Hollywood as Industry", in John Hill and Pamela Church Gibson (eds.), *American Cinema and Hollywood: Critical Approaches* (Oxford: Oxford University Press, 2000), 25.
7. Gomery, "Hollywood as Industry", 21–3.
8. Earl Theisen, "The Evolution of the Motion Picture Story, Part II", *The International Photographer*, vol. 8, no. 4 (1936), 12.
9. Illustrated in David Robinson, *Georges Méliès: Father of Film Fantasy* (London: Museum of the Moving Image, 1993), 36; Richard Abel, *The Ciné Goes to Town: French Cinema 1896–1914* Revised Edition (London: University of California Press, 1998), 74–75.
10. Patrick Robertson, *Guinness Film Facts and Feats* (London: Guinness Books, 1985), 157.
11. Robertson, *Guinness Film*, 157.
12. David Bordwell, Janet Staiger, and Kristin Thompson, *The Classical Hollywood Cinema: Film Style and Mode of*

Production to 1960 (London: Routledge, 1985), 321.

13. Bordwell, Staiger, and Thompson, *Classical*, 26.

14. McKay, *Amateur Movie Making*, 183.

15. Phil Hardy (ed.), *The Aurum Film Encyclopedia: Horror* (London: Aurum Press, 1985), 40.

16. Grady Johnson, "Credits Ledger: Film Title-Making is Inventive Business", *New York Times*, 16 October 1955, X6.

17. Barry Salt, *Film Style and Technology: History and Analysis*, Second Edition (London: Starword, 1992), 189.

18. Johnson, "Credits Ledger", X6.

19. Johnson, "Credits Ledger", X6.

20. Deborah Allison, "Novelty Title Sequences and Self-Reflexivity in Classical Hollywood Cinema", *Screening the Past*, issue 20 (2006), http://www.screeningthepast.com/issue-20-first-release/novelty-title-sequences-and-self-reflexivity-in-classical-hollywood-cinema/.

21. Salt, *Film Style*, 210.

22. Johnson, "Credits Ledger", X6.

23. Gladwin Hill, "Screening the Movies' 'Main Titles'", *New York Times*, 7 June 1953, X4.

24. New York Times, "Howard Da Silva Loses Film Credit", *New York Times*, 26 April 1951, 34.

25. Paul Mayersberg, *Hollywood the Haunted House* (Harmondsworth: Penguin Books, 1967), 124.

26. Andrew Dowdy, *The Films of the Fifties: The American State of Mind* (New York: William Morrow, 1973), 43–44.

27. Pat Kirkham, "Looking for the Simple Idea", *Sight & Sound* vol. 4, no. 2, February 1994, 16.

28. Bordwell, Staiger, and Thompson, *Classical*, 247.

29. Kirkham, "Looking", 16.

30. Kirkham, "Looking", 16.

31. Dean Billanti, "The Names Behind the Titles", *Film Comment*, vol. 18, no. 3 (1982), 60.

32. Deborah Allison, "Do Not Forsake Me: The Ballad of *High Noon* and the Rise of the Movie Theme Song", *Senses of Cinema*, no. 28 (2003), https://www.sensesofcinema.com/2003/cinema-and-music/ballad_of_high_noon/.

33. Writers Guild of America, *Theatrical and Television Basic*

Agreement (1995), 261.
34. Herbert Muschamp, "Blueprint: The Shock of the Familiar", *New York Times Magazine*, 13 December 1998, https://www.nytimes.com/1998/12/13/magazine/blueprint-the-shock-of-the-familiar.html.
35. Joe Shepter, "Imaginary Forces", *Adobe Motion Gallery*, www.adobe.co.uk/motion/gallery/imgforces/main.html (accessed 10 August 2005; page now discontinued).
36. Katie Makal, "Digital Domain Animates *Fight Club* Titles", *Design in Motion*, 24 November 1999, http://DesigninMotion.com/.getarticle/.378231349 (accessed 1 September 2001; page now discontinued).

First published in *Film International* (online edition), 30 January 2011. http://filmint.nu/?p=202.

NOVELTY TITLE SEQUENCES AND SELF-REFLEXIVITY IN CLASSICAL HOLLYWOOD CINEMA

There were things that could be done with film,
it was crazy not to do them.

—title designer Wayne Fitzgerald[1]

In 1976 Saul Bass designed the opening title sequence for *That's Entertainment, Part II* (Gene Kelly) and in doing so created a piece of film that was about title sequences, as well as being one itself. The film's compilation format of classic clips from Hollywood musicals inspired him to emulate a wide-ranging series of titles from the classical period and, in particular, the 1930s. The result is a joyous celebration of a range of titling styles designed to entertain in their own right, sometimes imitating existing sequences, and sometimes inspired by what Bass calls the "mythic memory" of sequences that could, or should, have been.[2]

This sequence highlights two important issues. In its pastiche of title sequences from the 1930s it shows some of the sorts of novelty sequences produced at that time. It is historically important to remember that such sequences existed since many of the journalistic articles written about film titles in recent years present an inaccurate picture proposing that film titling was universally dull and conservative until 1954 when the form was revolutionised by Bass in his design for Otto Preminger's *Carmen Jones*. Typical of such articles is David Thomson's, which claims that, "For decades before the 1950s, movie credits had meekly followed whatever standard treatment prevailed at every studio. [...] The music over the credits sometimes had the mood of the picture to come, but the graphics themselves were classical lettering on a bland background".[3] As I will show, the history of title sequences is far more lively and varied than this.

The second issue relates to what is often perceived as a key purpose of title design, namely finding ways to prepare the viewer for the experience of watching the coming film. In *That's Entertainment, Part II*, pleasure and function are seamlessly blended in a sequence that names the film, credits the cast, hints at what will follow, and sets an appropriate tone—as well as providing a stylistic history lesson. David Geffner has argued that title sequences "form a kind of contract, outlining the filmmaker's intentions and, for better or worse, setting up expectations that the audience, almost subliminally, will demand to be met".[4] This attitude can be discerned in the design of many sequences described in this article, but I will also show that in other sequences the importance of this function is displaced by other features. Indeed, the common factor of the sequences featured here is a flamboyant exhibitionism that revels in its own cleverness. In this respect, these sequences differ considerably from the attitudes to film titling that later rose to dominance.

Experimentation with striking and unusual title sequences began as early as the late 1910s, but it was the 1930s when an explosion of ideas and techniques occurred that consolidated the role of the title sequence as something more than a list of names. A wide range of styles and techniques were used at this time, many of them indigenous to the period. Although many sequences were designed with relative stylistic economy, others seemed fascinated instead with the potential of the medium for exploring techniques of direct address and self-reflexivity. These highlight a more than usually complex relationship between themselves, the main part of the film they introduce and the process of its production.

In this article I explore a selection of sequences that foreground the problematic relationship between the exhibitionism of title sequences and the need to construct a full diegesis. All of these sequences are self-reflexive, a process normally manifested through the introduction of film titles into the diegetic space, or through references made to them either by fictional characters in the film or a member of the production crew.

Such a collapsing of the boundaries between the diegetic and non-diegetic space contravenes a convention that many theorists, such as Bordwell, Staiger, and Thompson, have looked upon as central to the 'classical style', although these authors acknowledge that exceptions exist.[5] This convention is that the diegetic space should be internally coherent and that filmic technique should not conspicuously impinge upon it. These sequences raise questions about such ways of understanding the construction and pleasures of Hollywood cinema. Are title sequences an entirely different medium from the films they introduce, or does their failure to conceal their artifice, and their frequent promotion of non-narrative pleasures, represent an intensification of a more widespread mode of film practice in which a narrative structure and apparently seamless diegetic construct exist merely as an organisational principle in which other pleasures are contained?

Many films of the studio era, and indeed the majority of films now, do indeed tend to avoid actively drawing attention to the fact that the diegetic space is an artificial entity constructed in the process of the film's production. Perhaps the most notable exception to this rule is film comedy. Henry Jenkins has argued that, "the comic film tended to lag behind the rest of American cinema in its acceptance of classical Hollywood norms, remaining one of the places where marginal film practices enjoyed the greatest acceptability".[6] Steve Seidman's excellent study of comedian comedy cites a wide range of instances where diegetic boundaries have been rendered problem-atic, and one of the foremost sites he identifies for using such a device is the opening (or sometimes the end) credits sequence.[7]

The practice of foregrounding the process of production is a feature also found in many avant-garde films. It is not unusual for the materiality of the title cards to be emphasised in such films, as lettering is scratched or painted on film, inscribed onto a physical object, or cards are positioned or removed by hand. Examples can be seen in *Color Cry* (Len Lye, 1953), *Little Stabs at Happiness* (Ken Jacobs, 1959–63), and *Gulls and Buoys* (Robert Breer, 1974). Moreover, title sequences that rely heavily upon cinematic trickery show a preoccupation that Tom Gunning has observed in the writings of the early modernists, namely "a fascination with the potential of the medium".[8] Observing that one feature of early cin-ema and the avant-garde alike is "its freedom from the creation of a diegesis, its accent on direct stimulation", Gunning identifies a sensibility that he terms "the cinema of attraction".[9] The attitude that he describes can be seen to resonate through the titling innovations of films cited in this essay.

Although there are parallels between such instances and features of some mainstream comedies, we should be wary of inferring too close a commonality between the two forms. Steve Neale and Frank Krutnik have argued that "neither comedy nor the comic can be regarded as inherently subversive or progressive, or as inherently avant-garde [... since] the level of generic verisimilitude [in expecting the unexpected] accounts [...] for the *non* avant-garde character of even the most formally adventurous comedies".[10] Accepting the validity of their argument, we can nonetheless recognise that in some of the title sequences this essay describes, features strongly associated with both classical film comedy and avant-garde cinema are brought together.

Some of the sequences I will describe are from comedies, and in these we can detect some strong consistencies between the title sequence and the rest of the film in the ways in which the viewer is addressed. Most of them are from other genres, though, and would therefore seem to be at odds with the films they introduce. Even if we allow that title sequences, like certain film genres, are a site in which self-reflexive devices have been normalised, we are still left with a situation where the artificiality of the film construct is highlighted to a degree that raises questions about the validity of arguments which hold that mainstream films, of the classical period at least, do all they can to present themselves as hermetically sealed entities.

THE VARYING RELATIONSHIPS BETWEEN TITLE SEQUENCES AND THE DIEGESIS

The self-reflexive sequences discussed in this essay can be placed into three basic categories. The first two are quite similar to each other in that they both involve titles inscribed onto physical objects. In the first case there is the insinuation that these objects may belong within the diegetic space but are not unequivocally placed there. In the second group are sequences where the credit titles are inarguably placed within that space. The third group involves some interaction between the credit titles and either the characters in the film or its production crew. Perhaps the most interesting feature of these sequences is the range of ways in which they call into question the nature of the diegesis and the means by which the films structure and present this organisational system.

Traditionally, credit titles have collided with the diegetic image in one of two ways. Either the whole sequence has been marked off from the diegesis by placing the lettering on a totally different background, such as a plain board or piece of paper, or else the lettering has been superimposed over diegetic footage without any attempt to conceal the independence of one plane from the other, or to conjoin them in such a way as to suggest that their origins might be linked. The films described below provide exceptions to this rule.

Defining the boundaries of the diegesis can be a difficult task in itself, although the meaning of the term seems fairly straightforward at first glance. For a popular textbook definition we may as well take the one provided by Bordwell and Thompson in *Film Art*: "In a narrative film, the world of the film's story. The diegesis includes events that are presumed to have occurred and actions and spaces not shown onscreen."[11] When a film opens, the viewer has no frame of reference, however. How is s/he supposed to assess the status of the background image during a title sequence that comes right at the beginning of a film, as many of them do? If the background is plain, or a painted picture, then knowledge of convention may suggest that after the titles there will be a cut to a live-action scene that has no spatial link to the title card. Yet as I will later describe, *Whirlpool* (Otto Preminger, 1950), provides one exemplary illustration of just how easily the viewer can be tricked.

Live-action backgrounds and the presence of three-dimensional objects during the titles present a greater problem for the viewer. A comparison of three title sequences, which share strong similarities with each other, will illustrate this difficulty: *My Darling Clementine* (John Ford, 1946), *The Cat and the Fiddle* (Lloyd Bacon, 1933), and *You'll Never Get Rich* (Sidney Lanfield, 1941). These belong to a small but diverse group of films that present their opening titles on billboards or signposts. To illustrate the point in hand, the pertinent feature of these sequences is the varying relation between the signposts and/or billboards in the title sequence and the space of the subsequent film.

My Darling Clementine uses titles scorched into a single wooden signpost. This is the only physical object in the frame during the title sequence, which ends with a cut. There is therefore no suggestion that the post is located anywhere within the diegetic space (save only that its style suggests rural origins). *The Cat and the Fiddle* shows cars circling a roundabout, in the centre of which is a notice board that a man approaches. We see that it displays a poster advertising Ramon Novarro and Jeannette McDonald in *The Cat and the Fiddle*. The camera tracks into this poster and freezes, after which the board rotates to show two further posters/title cards. As in *My Darling Clementine*, a cut is used to separate the title sequence from the rest of the movie. *You'll Never Get Rich* is by far the most elaborate of the three sequences. It shows a man being chauffeured along a country road. The passenger asks the driver to slow down

You'll Never Get Rich (1941)

as, watching from the window, he sees a row of signs along the roadside on which there appear film credits as well as pictures of the top-billed stars. Presently credit titles start to appear on fences and buildings too. After the last one, the film cuts back to the passenger, who tells his driver, "All right, go ahead. Thank you." At this point, as in the other sequences, the film cuts to a different location. It is a city scene and is therefore evidently a different space. Yet a street sign passed by a car establishes this new location, the iconography of the shot thus linking it to the previous sequence.

In these films, we see three examples of titles inscribed upon physical objects that have no clear spatial link to the actual space in which the narrative occurs. There is a gradation between the first sequence, which is completely divorced from any narrative space, and the second, which suggests a similarity between the space of the titles and the following scenes by including some action in the title sequence. In the final example, there is a strong continuity with the construction of the subsequent space and action, due to the presence of dialogue and a minimal narrative content during the titles as well as loose graphic matching between the two spaces. Although in all these examples a cut separates the space of the titles from the main part of the film, some films discussed later in the essay proceed without any intermediary cut. Instead of being insinuated into a mock-diegetic space, their titles are patently positioned within the very space where the narrative action occurs.

TITLES INSINUATED INTO THE DIEGETIC SPACE

The practice of inscribing titles onto physical objects positioned outside the diegetic space is most commonly associated with the trick and novelty title sequences of the 1930s. The sequences discussed in this section are designed in such a way as to suggest the possibility that the space presented may be diegetic though. Instead of using motionless two-dimensional artwork—a far more common technique of the era—they use live-action backgrounds that do indeed turn out to have strong graphic connections with spaces seen subsequently.

One of the sequences that most successfully insinuates titles into the diegetic space without ever framing them in the same shot as the narrative action is *The Great Ziegfeld* (Robert Z. Leonard, 1936). Its titles are spelled out in lights on a large and elaborate scaffolding structure across which the camera pans, pausing briefly on each set of titles. A cut at the end of the sequence provides the transition to the first unambiguously diegetic location: a fairground at night. The nocturnal setting and elaborate incandescent structures of the carnival park are sufficiently similar to the illuminated titles to erode the boundaries between the two spaces.

Boy Meets Girl (Lloyd Bacon, 1938) uses the device of a book to create a visual continuity between its opening title sequence and the diegetic space. A technique used in several films, here the book is on the very verge of placement within the diegetic space. Although it does not appear in any scene of narrative action, it is discovered through a track-in to a desk artistically littered with miscellaneous items including a typewriter and several spilling film cans that mark the location as a screenwriter's office. This, of course, is a film about screenwriters. In case the other clues leave any doubt remaining, the document is entitled, "Final Script", with the film's main title and credits revealed on the inside pages.

In other sequences, we discover the credit titles in slightly less expected places than the relatively popular sites of signposts, billboards, or book pages. Most of these sequences are enormously inventive. One example of a stock trick-title sequence can be seen in *Her Man* (Tay Garnett, 1930), where titles scraped into sand are washed away by incoming waves. *Maytime* (Robert Z. Leonard, 1937) provides another charming example. In this sequence two techniques are used. For the first and last groups of titles, blossom petals fall from a tree onto the surface of a running stream. There they form the letters of the titles before dispersing with the movement of the water. Intermediate titles are cut into the bark of the tree trunk. Explicit homage was paid to this sequence in the titles for *That's Entertainment, Part II*, which also included a variant on waves washing titles from the sand, although Bass admitted that he had not seen *Her Man* or indeed any other film using the device.[12] A handful of similar, but more crudely executed examples can be found in later years. For *Ali Baba and the Forty Thieves* (Arthur Lubin, 1944), titles painted on a wall are doused by upturned water jars. In *Joan of Paris* (Robert Stevenson, 1942), when a waiter opens a champagne bottle with an audible pop, its content brims over, acting as wipes (through a rather crude cheating) between the sets of titles that seem to be printed on the bottle label. These films differ from such examples as *The Great Ziegfeld* and *The Cat and the Fiddle* in so far as the act of removing the credits means that they have to be miraculously re-placed somehow. If the more perfectly realised examples, such as *Maytime*, instil a sense of the marvellous, in other cases the crudity of the cinematic trickery used to achieve this effect can be destructive of the illusion that the credits somehow appear in 'real' space and time. The separation between the space of the title sequences and the subsequent action is thus defined not only by editorial strategy but also by perceptual factors centred upon the verisimilitude of the illusion.

TITLES POSITIONED WITHIN THE DIEGETIC SPACE

Some films unquestionably inscribe their titles into the diegetic space by positioning the text as part of the scenery in which the action occurs, occasionally proceeding without even a cut at the end of the sequence. *Whirlpool* provides an example that is both unusual and immensely effective. The opening titles appear in black upon an almost neutral background, which is decorated only by a very faint repeating pattern. The pattern crawls upward at the same pace as the lettering, rendering beyond doubt the fact that the text is not superimposed but painted upon it. After the final credit, a swish-pan takes us all the way back up the paper to the start of the credits list, although motion blur means that the titles are not legible during this return journey. As the paper crumples up, it becomes evident that it belongs to a roll of wrapping paper handled by a shop assistant. The shot has proceeded from the credit list to the shop girl without any visible intermediary cut. The most curious feature of this sequence is not its placement of titles on a material that is indisputably part of the diegetic world but rather the postponement of this discovery until after the opening titles have ended.

Where the Sidewalk Ends (Otto Preminger, 1950) provides another interesting example in a film by the same director. The movie opens with titles hand-painted on a sidewalk, seen under the feet of a man who walks across them. A second man lingers with his feet upon the main title before the camera pans with him as he steps off the edge of the pavement and over a rivulet of water pouring into the gutter. Although there is editing in the sequence, which includes action and diegetic sound, the space of the sidewalk is clearly consistent with continued footage of the city during a rainy night.

Some sequences use for their main title what we might call a 'found artefact'—an object that exists elsewhere in the filmic space and which names the film—thereby obviating the necessity of creating a specific title card. One such instance can be found in *Verboten!* (Samuel Fuller, 1959), in which a group of American soldiers discuss the meaning of the word, which appears on a signpost. A similar device is used in *Sunset Boulevard* (Billy Wilder, 1950), where the main title is painted onto a kerbstone, an already existent street sign that may feasibly have existed as an artefact outside the film as well as within it. *Portrait of Jennie* (William Dieterle, 1948) is limited to a single title, this time shown as a picture gallery catalogue entry—"Portrait of Jennie, dated 1934, h.30: w.25 inches"—the image accompanied by a spoken discussion of the painting. Each of these sequences achieves an interesting subversion of the normal relationship between title sequences and the films they introduce without employing the levels of flamboyant cinematic trickery that were seen with relative regularity in 1930s cinema.

INTERACTION BETWEEN TITLES AND CHARACTERS OR CREW

Some films go further yet and depict the very act of creating the titles. As the process of writing is made visible, the act of directly addressing the audience is emphasised and the narration foregrounded. One example from the golden age of novelty title sequences is *Carefree* (Mark Sandrich, 1938). In that film, a white background is covered over with streaky black paint, in which a finger traces the credits. The lettering is then scrubbed out by a pair of hands before the finger writes out the next set. A range of decorative patterns are created as the titles are erased by different hand movements each time. *I Love Melvin* (Don Weis, 1953) provides a significant variation on the idea in that the author of the titles is identified. The film's star, Debbie Reynolds, is shown dressed in a ballet costume and looking into a dressing room mirror in order to apply her lipstick. Her reflection catches the eye of the camera. She smiles, her mirror image looking straight at the audience, and writes the main title in red lipstick on the glass.

Perhaps the most interesting feature of this particular sequence is that, at this point in the film, Debbie Reynolds can be read as appearing in her purest form—as herself, as a star. She has not yet fully taken on the role of her fictional character in the film, although she is dressed for the part. The way that her eye catches the camera so that she appears to look straight at the audience circumvents

I Love Melvin (1953)

any fictional distance and allows us to imagine that it is Reynolds, not her character, addressing us with her stare. Her act of applying lipstick also suggests the preparation for a performance rather than the performance itself. By such means, the transition between the film's production process and its fiction is made manifest, not least through the process of writing the titles before our very eyes.

To Kill a Mockingbird (Robert Mulligan, 1962) handles the interaction between character and titles in a slightly different fashion. The film begins with a child's hands opening a box, which contains all sorts of oddments. This, we learn later in the film, is Scout's treasure chest. Scout, unseen in this sequence except for her hands, sings to herself as she removes a crayon from the box and starts to colour over a sheet of white paper, which reveals the main title. The fact that in this sequence the character is responsible for making visible the title, rather than actually writing it as a communication to the viewer, is a significant difference from *Carefree* and *I Love Melvin*. The lettering is something that is already there for her to discover. Another hand can be detected therefore: that of the filmmaker who has set the scene.

There are also many films in which the act of inscription may not be visible but where characters interact with the titles. Since this invariably produces a humorous effect, it is normally used in film comedies although there are occasional exceptions to this rule. Using credit titles as comic props has particular associations with animation. The most famous examples are surely *The Pink Panther* (Blake Edwards, 1963) and its sequels, which show the Panther toying with the letters, just as the anthropomorphised letters sometimes toy with him, as when his wolf whistle at Claudia Cardinale's title provokes a hand to appear from the credit in order to issue a resounding slap. Earlier and equally entertaining examples exist, though. One of those went so far as to create its main titles out of the characters themselves. In *Abbott and Costello Meet Frankenstein* (Charles T. Barton, 1948), two skeletons (one short and fat, one tall and thin—the proportions of the stars) collide with one another when running frantically from Frankenstein's monster. This mishap causes the complete collapse of their frames into separate bones arranged as words. In films such as these, which are live action bar the credits, there is clearly no blurring of diegetic boundaries, but merely a subversion of the credit titles' normal form and purpose. There are also some live-action title sequences that do similar things, however, and these are more problematic in terms of actors slipping back and forth between a plainly narrative role and an ambiguous status somewhere between character and star. Indeed, interaction between actors or characters and title lettering is often accompanied by a direct address to the audience, just as Debbie Reynolds catches the eye of the camera in *I Love Melvin.*

One film where this occurs is *The Court Jester* (Norman Panama and Melvin Frank, 1955). Its title sequence is dominated by Danny Kaye's performance of a song discussing salient features of the forthcoming movie whilst choreographing the appearance, disappearance, and motion of some of the titles through his own movements. Another interesting sequence introduces *Will Success Spoil Rock Hunter?* (Frank Tashlin, 1957), which opens with an extreme long shot of a one-man orchestra playing all the instruments for the Twentieth Century Fox fanfare. A closer shot shows him to be the star of the film, Tony Randall, who introduces himself to the audience. Credits materialise as he clicks his fingers, but his frequent mistakes cause the wrong titles to appear so that he eventually screws his notes up in frustration. At one stage, he announces, "The title of this movie is *The Girl Can't Help It.* No—we made that!" This is the first of several references to the director's earlier releases that punctuate a film that is extremely self-reflexive throughout.

Self-reflexive jokes in title sequences normally involve the titles themselves in some way, although this is not

Will Success Spoil Rock Hunter? (1957)

always the case. One very original variant occurs in *Monkey Business* (Howard Hawks, 1952). In this sequence we hear the voice of director, although the only direct address to the audience is in the standard function of the titles themselves. There is no physical or verbal interaction between character and lettering. Nevertheless, there is a confusion of the boundaries between diegetic and non-diegetic space and, perhaps more interestingly, a literalising of the function of the title sequence as an opening, a transition into the diegetic world. In *Monkey Business*, the diegesis breaks in on the non-diegetic space. The background shows a still photograph of the front of a house, its front door squarely facing the camera. Whilst we soon discover that this image is diegetic, at first it seems as flat as the title lettering so that the status of the image is initially questionable. The otherwise conventional unrolling of the credits in superimposition upon this flat, unassuming backdrop is interrupted twice as the door opens from within and Cary Grant emerges, shifting the image into three-dimensionality. The director's voice interjects, "Not yet, Cary!"—significantly using the actor rather than the character name. Each time this happens, Grant retreats into the house and closes the door behind him. At the end of the sequence, he makes an identical entrance and this time the film is allowed to progress.

In foregrounding the act of direct address and, in some cases, showing the real or ostensible origin of the credit titles, the sequences described in this essay highlight, to varying degrees, the act of showmanship involved in introducing a film to its audience. Perhaps more significantly, they sometimes go so far as to emphasise that the film is indeed just a film. It is show, an illusion forged of the same materials as the titles themselves. This is a message made manifest in those titles that intrude into the diegetic space or even, as in the case of *Monkey Business*, a diegesis that intrudes into the space of the titles.

It might be argued that there is nothing particularly distinguished about this feature. Many films, even so-called classical films, have self-reflexive moments, or characters that seem to burst out of the diegetic space to perform for the viewer, seemingly unmediated by plot and character—a common feature of musical numbers, for instance. Indeed, since it is comedies and musicals that seemingly have the least regard for the proprieties of 'classicism', it is hardly surprising that many of the most extreme examples of using titles as objects and violating the diegetic boundaries have been found in these genres. The opposing logic of real-world laws and cinematic possibilities provides the meat of the joke. Nevertheless, the non-comic effect of this process in films such as *Where the Sidewalk Ends* and *Verboten!* at least indicates that in the title sequences of film genres more circumscribed by the constraints of 'classical Hollywood' convention, the level of experimentation permitted by comedy is not entirely excluded.

The legitimisation of a whole range of styles and techniques can be partly explained by the fact that the presence of the written titles (and they are almost always written) delays the moment at which the viewer can be psychologically sucked into the diegetic world, unhampered by overt narrational marks.[13] The way that the credits announce the film crew, and the stars in particular, also means that they refer directly to elements external to the film, so that title sequences have sometimes been written about as existing within the domain of what Gerard Genette has called 'paratext', which mediates between text and extratext, that is between diegetic elements and external features.[14] Already appealing to the audience directly by virtue of the title lettering, and by the promotion of extratextual features, some films seek to make the most of the opportunities offered by the impossibility of showing only a diegesis and to make a feature of their exhibitionism instead. Such an attitude has helped to render the title sequence a site in which the usual 'rules' of mainstream film do not apply, in which 'anything goes'. In an era when the innovations of title designers before Saul Bass have come to be largely overlooked, the long-standing exploration of the different possible relationships between title sequences and the films they introduce deserves to be reappraised.

NOTES

1. Wayne Fitzgerald interviewed in Dean Billanti, "The Names Behind the Titles", *Film Comment*, vol. 18, no. 3, May/June 1982, 68.
2. Saul Bass, "The 'Compleat Film-Maker'—from Titles to Features", *American Cinematographer*, vol. 58, no. 3, March 1977, 290.
3. David Thomson, "The Man with the Golden Pen", *Independent on Sunday* (London), 21 June 1998, 19.
4. David Geffner, "First Things First", *Filmmaker Magazine*, vol. 6, no. 1, fall 1997, https://www.filmmakermagazine.com/archives/issues/fall1997/firstthingsfirst.php.
5. David Bordwell, Janet Staiger, and Kristin Thompson, *The Classical Hollywood Cinema: Film Style and Mode of Production to 1960* (London: Routledge, 1985), 21–22.
6. Henry Jenkins III, "Fifi was My Mother's Name!: Anarchistic Comedy, the Vaudeville Aesthetic, and *Diplomaniacs*", *Velvet Light Trap*, no. 27, fall 1990, 9.
7. Steve Seidman, *Comedian Comedy: A Tradition in Hollywood Film* (Ann Arbor: UMI Research Press, 1981), esp. 34–35.
8. Tom Gunning, "The Cinema of Attraction: Early Film, its Spectator and the Avant-Garde", *Wide Angle*, vol. 8, no. 3/4, fall 1986, 64.
9. Gunning, "The Cinema of Attraction", 66.

10. Steve Neale and Frank Krutnik, *Popular Film and Television Comedy* (London: Routledge, 1990), 93–94.
11. David Bordwell and Kristin Thompson, *Film Art: An Introduction* (New York: Alfred A. Knopf, 1986), 385.
12. Bass, "The 'Compleat Film-Maker'", 290.
13. A handful of films in this period made use of spoken or sung credits, such as *Sweet Rosie O'Grady* (Irving Cummings, 1943), *Meet Me After the Show* (Richard Sale, 1951), and *Road to Bali* (Hal Walker, 1952), although these normally occurred simultaneously with written titles, as they did in these examples. Orson Welles famously spoke the credits to *The Magnificent Ambersons* (Orson Welles, 1942), but did so at the end rather than the beginning of the film, which opened with only two brief title cards.
14. For an example of this approach, see Leopold Joseph Charney, *Just Beginnings: Film Studies, Close Analysis and the Viewer's Experience* (Ann Arbor: UMI, 1993).

First published as "Innovative Vorspanne und Reflexivität im klassischen Hollywoodkino", in Alexander Böhnke, Rembert Hüser, and Georg Stanitzek (eds.), *Das Buch zum Vorspanne: 'The Title is a Shot'* (Berlin: Vorwerk 8, 2006), 90–101, translated from English to German by Andrea Kirchhartz. First published in English language with minor revisions in *Screening the Past*, issue 20 (2006). http://www.screeningthepast.com/issue-20-first-release/novelty-title-sequences-and-self-reflexivity-in-classical-hollywood-cinema/.

YOU OUGHTA BE IN PICTURES: CARTOONS AND CARICATURES IN OPENING TITLE SEQUENCES

What links Laurel and Hardy character dolls, the *St. Trinian's* books, lazy film producers, Dick Tracy newspaper strips, and *The Pink Panther Show*? Well, for one thing, they all reference or are referenced by opening title sequences of live-action feature films. Why, and to what ends? Now, that's going to require a slightly longer answer...

TITLE SEQUENCES AS PARATEXTS

One fruitful way of approaching this question is to consider the title sequences I discuss here—all of which feature cartoons or caricatures of actors, characters, and/or members of the production crew—in the context of paratexts. This term, coined by Gerard Genette, refers to elements existing in the zone immediately adjacent to what is often thought of as the 'main text' or 'body' of a work. This approach can aid an understanding of how our experience of specific works—in this instance, popular movies—can be shaped by liminal elements that forge intimate connections with a host of other cultural touchstones.

There is a growing scholarly tendency to frame title sequences within this context, although it is worth noting that they occupy an unusual position in the wider realm of paratexts. Unlike posters, trailers, critical reviews, or novelisations, for instance, title sequences are designed to be consumed together with the 'main text' whereas these other groups are designed to be experienced separately. They are, essentially, more elaborate versions of the subcategory of paratexts that Genette called the 'peritext', which (as he describes in relation to printed books) may include such elements as the names of the author(s) and publisher, the title of the work, a likeness of the author, and genre indication.[1]

In many cases (and in almost all cases during the first few decades of feature film production) they are also what Jonathan Gray has aptly dubbed 'entryway paratexts', which "try to control the viewer's entrance to the text".[2] Indeed, the practice of viewing title sequences entirely apart from the films or television works to which they belong only started to gain a notable foothold in the 1990s when they became a topic for illustrated lectures, gallery exhibitions and, increasingly, online video playlists.

As peritexts, nearly all opening title sequences include some combination of production company logos and/or credits to individual cast and crew. Some also divulge the film's origin in a book, play, radio serial, or newspaper story, or announce the supply of costumes and props by upmarket jewellers or fashion houses. In such ways, they invariably point to bodies external to the film or television program they introduce. This is necessitated by obligations to trade union agreements and individual contracts, of course, but it also serves another important function—to shape, and often enhance, the viewers' anticipation of the experience to come. This role is often performed in conjunction with additional textual elements such as music, typographic style, and other visual imagery—all of which can conjure their own sets of associations.

In this essay, I explore this process via a close look at a very specific subset of film title sequences. As well as including the names of production personnel in written form, in this group the credits are supplemented by cartoons or caricatures. Like the written credits, this is a direct form of address to the audience that sits outside the diegesis. What interests me about these sequences is how they talk to us about the star image and wider careers of the performers, or about reassuringly familiar narrative structures, generic stereotypes, and cultural products, or else reinforce popular myths about the role and characterisation of various members of the crew.

The sequences I discuss are drawn from British and American cinema and, in most cases, were produced between the 1930s and 1950s. While the national boundaries are simply drawn according to the limits of my research, the date range reflects the preponderance of this kind of title sequence within a particular era. As I documented in a previous essay for *Film International*, title sequences featuring one or more still pictures were at the height of their popularity during this period, after which title backgrounds incorporating at least some degree of narrative action eclipsed their dominance.[3] A few of the sequences I discuss are animated, but this technique was relatively rare. There is also a third characteristic uniting the sequences I discuss—namely, genre. Virtually all these films are comedies of some kind, whether slapstick, romantic, musical, horror, or some combination thereof.

THE ACTORS

Cartoons and caricatures of actors appear in opening title sequences in various forms. Some present a simple, single image that appears briefly on just one title card; in others the image remains on screen throughout the sequence. By contrast, some feature still or animated images exhibiting varying degrees of technical and narrative complexity. In many cases the caricatures are drawn or painted, while others employ photography of three-dimensional models.

The most notable thing they have in common is that the caricatures of the actors are instantly recognisable— or would have been intended as such for contemporary audiences. Most modern film fans should have little difficulty identifying the caricatured subjects in *Block-Heads* (John G. Blystone, 1938), *Never Give a Sucker an Even Break* (Edward Cline, 1941), or *Pat and Mike* (George Cukor, 1952) as Laurel and Hardy, W. C. Fields, and Spencer Tracy and Katharine Hepburn respectively. By contrast, it seems likely that a much-diminished fan base will now seize upon the comic sketch that graces the opening titles of *Sh! The Octopus* (William McGann, 1937) as depicting the once-popular comedians Hugh Herbert and Allen Jenkins. Happily, those actors' names are there in writing too; they even score a billing hat trick as the sequence also includes labelled photographic close-ups of them.

So what's the point of including cartoons as well as written credits? Above all, these images reference, and contribute to, the carefully cultivated star personas of the actors. Take the example of *Never Give a Sucker an Even Break.* Its title sequence features a short animation of a sour-faced, bulbous-nosed, cane-wielding, cigar-chomping fat man suffering the distress of a waistcoat

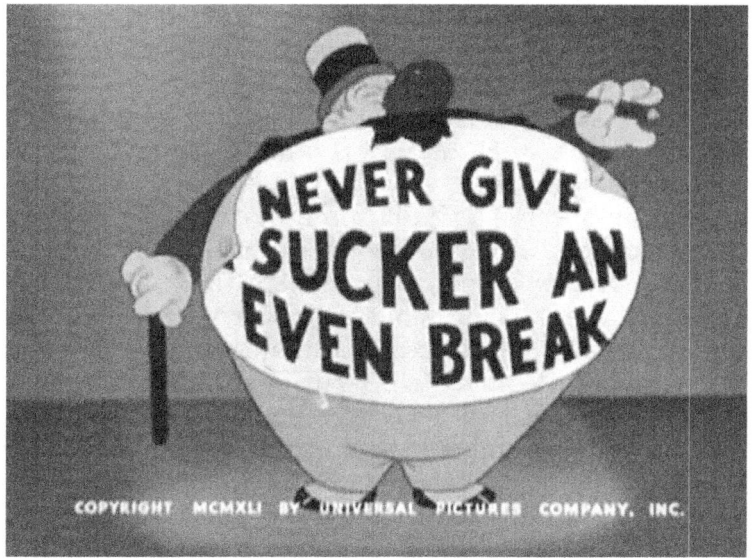

Never Give a Sucker an Even Break (1941)

that busts open as his stomach expands until the movie title can be clearly read emblazoned across his enormous belly. It's no matter that the character's facial features can barely be seen behind the big clown-style nose; there are ample cues to associate it with Fields' star image. His previous movie, *The Bank Dick* (Edward Cline, 1940), had also caricatured him in its title sequence. There was no animation in that one, but the cigar, the nose, and the belly were all present in spades. A little earlier still was *You Can't Cheat an Honest Man* (George Marshall, 1939). There he appeared as a three-dimensional figurine—with the iconic nose, cane, and cigar (though a bit less of a belly)—as the main title was hauled up on a flag behind him. Caricatures of Fields featuring the same trademark visual cues can also be found in film posters, newspapers and magazines, and other contemporary paratexts, extending his position from performer to cultural product. Decades after his death this cartoon imagery remained potent enough to feature in posters, televised advertisements, and collectable merchandise for corn chips, when the Fritos brand adopted Fields as their mascot in 1972.[4]

We can observe a similar process operating in other title sequences. The cartoons of Laurel and Hardy found in *Block-Heads* reflect and augment the many caricatures of these stars locatable in a range of toys, figurines, and decorative homewares, not to mention their regular appearance in comic strip form in the British weekly paper *Film Fun* and elsewhere during the 1930s and beyond. While the other most fondly remembered comedy team of '30s and '40s Hollywood, The Marx Brothers, never made it into regular comic strip form, the plethora of cartoon images on their movie posters and other marketing materials links closely with the caricatures so regularly featured in the title sequences to their films. *At the Circus* (Edward Buzzell, 1939), *Go West* (Edward Buzzell, 1940), and *The Big Store* (Charles Reisner, 1941) all supply examples.

Returning, for a moment, to Fields—it is worth noting that despite the very similar ways in which he is depicted in the title sequences of the three films cited above we also find a degree of variation tailored to the roles he plays in them. In each case, he appears in the costume of the character he will portray. Moreover, the unfurling of the banner in *You Can't Cheat an Honest Man* references the showmanship of his character of a circus operator, linking the title sequence even more closely to the film at large. This practice was widespread and, as a way of preparing the audience for the upcoming diegesis, was leaned on particularly heavily outside of 'comedian comedy' films.

Not all actors caricatured in opening title sequences

are known solely for their comedy roles. A small handful of the many films giving their stars this treatment are *Nothing Sacred* (William A. Wellman, 1937) starring Carole Lombard and Frederic March, *The Baroness and the Butler* (Walter Lang, 1938) starring William Powell and Annabella, *No Time for Comedy* (William Keighley, 1940) starring Rosalind Russell and James Stewart, and *Presenting Lily Mars* (Norman Taurog, 1943) starring Judy Garland and Van Heflin. In films such as these, the caricatures serve to emphasise the comedic potential of the performers. These caricatures and, by implication, the movie actors/characters are witty; they allow the performers to bask in the glow of that wit before they've even been called upon to do anything. It's a great way to set the mood for the film and whet the anticipation of the audience.

Such sequences usually indicate the type of role the actors will play in the upcoming film as well as introducing stereotypical comic situations—often centring on a 'battle of the sexes' interplay between the male and female leads. There are also cases where the title sequence designers find clever and intriguing ways to comment on the stars' personas and/or their filmic roles without recourse to the usual conventions of direct visual caricature. One nice example is *Road to Rio* (Norman Z.

Road to Rio (1947)

McLeod, 1947). Here, Bing Crosby and Bob Hope's written credits dance a duet on stick-figure legs, before Dorothy Lamour's more shapely-legged credit inserts itself between them and barges her co-stars off screen. When they return and pile on top of her the encounter explodes into a chaotic scrum of disassembled letters, making way for the main title, which also boogies to the music. This sequence establishes the dynamic between the main characters, and the general tone of the film, in a clever and entertaining way.

THE CHARACTERS

As we have seen, it is common for title sequences featuring caricatures of actors to offer some indications of the story's setting or aspects of the plot, especially when the performers are associated with multiple genres. Providing this kind of preparatory information can play a valuable role in its own right, and there are actually far more films foreshadowing their characters in cartoon form than those caricaturing their actors.

In some cases, the narrative situations depicted offer a considerable quantity of information—sometimes going so far as to précis the plot. There are even rare examples of title sequences in which real-life public figures are caricatured—such as the cartoon images of Adolf Hitler in the Hal Roach Studio's short film *The Devil with Hitler* (Gordon Douglas, 1942) and its sequel featurette *Nazty Nuisance* (Glenn Tryon, 1943). In other title sequences, the cartoons are far more generic—pointing to the general milieu in which the story unfolds and, in such cases, often featuring stereotypical character types identifiable by uniforms or other distinctive costumes. In either case, the tendency is to highlight the film's genre, almost invariably comedy, while further narrowing the frame of reference to a particular sub-genre or oft-used narrative situation.

Take, for instance, *Girl Crazy* (Norman Taurog, 1943), in which we see a man come a-cropper from his womanising ways before he finds love in the final title card, or *Mother is a Freshman* (Lloyd Bacon, 1948), which places a grown woman in various college scenarios. There are no big spoilers here. The function these sequences fulfil is essentially similar to the trailers, marketing blurbs, and other promotional materials that place the film at hand within a particular cinematic niche. All these 'entryway' paratexts invoke other films as part of their pledge that the viewer will experience just the right degree of novelty within a reassuringly familiar framework.

In some films, the illustrative styles also reference other, non-cinematic, cultural products from which the films have been adapted or are otherwise aligned. Among the many screen spin-offs of the long-running Dick Tracy newspaper strip are four films produced by RKO: *Dick Tracy* (William Berke, 1945), *Dick Tracy vs. Cueball* (Gordon Douglas, 1946), *Dick Tracy's Dilemma* (John Rawlins, 1947), and *Dick Tracy Meets Gruesome* (John Rawlins, 1947). All feature variants of the same title sequence. They begin with a profile drawing of the famous sleuth before the camera pulls back to show the signature of the strip's creator, Chester Gould, at the bottom of the sketch. At the same time, the studio credit and main title slide into view from screen left. In each case, subsequent title cards feature drawings of other characters from the newspaper strip. Despite being filmed by three different directors, and the actor playing Tracy changing mid-way through this short series (with Morgan Conway replaced by Ralph Byrd—star of four earlier Dick Tracy film serials), their title sequences are remarkably uniform. Significantly, they all refer the viewer back to the newspaper strip, which they herald as the primary and definitive set of Tracy texts.

Over in the UK, a vogue for cartoon title sequences, which adorned several film series from the 1950s to the 1970s, was pre-empted by stand-alone school comedy *The Happiest Days of Your Life* (Frank Launder, 1950). This opened with a series of title cards drawn by the well-known British cartoonist Ronald Searle who, highly unusually for the time of production, received credit within the opening titles. Most contemporary viewers, in the UK at least, would doubtless have been familiar with his most famous creation: the *St. Trinian's* series of cartoons, which he had begun to produce in 1941—initially in magazines, and then in book form from 1948. Thus, this sequence held the promise of enjoyable school-

The Belles of St. Trinian's (1954)

set anarchy in a very similar vein to *St. Trinian's*. Later in the 1950s, Searle's series would itself be adapted for the screen. Here again, his title card illustrations for *The Belles of St. Trinian's* (Frank Launder, 1954), *Blue Murder at St. Trinian's* (Frank Launder, 1957), *The Pure Hell of St. Trinian's* (Frank Launder, 1960), and *The Great St. Trinian's Train Robbery* (Frank Launder and Sidney Gilliat, 1966) referred viewers back to his printed creations.

In the 1960s a rare reversal of this process occurred, with a cartoon character that first originated in movie title sequences spinning off into a long-running cartoon, and subsequent television, series accompanied by its own paratexts. Following widespread acclamation for Friz Freleng's Pink Panther, which riffed on the nickname of a stolen diamond in *The Pink Panther* (Blake Edwards, 1963), sequels *A Shot in the Dark* (Blake Edwards, 1964) and *Inspector Clouseau* (Bud Yorkin, 1968) pursued the same playful style but animated the character of Clouseau instead. The hapless detective would subsequently become as famous in his animated form as in his live-action incarnation.

THE CREW

Title sequences caricaturing the production crew are relatively rare, but are a lot of fun. Since the actors are invariably caricatured too there is some continuity in the internal logic and aesthetic cohesion of these sequences— yet the cartoons or caricatures of the crew function somewhat differently. Considered in terms of entryway paratexts, they do relatively little to usher the viewer into the diegetic world. Indeed, their effect is quite the opposite—emphasising instead the circumstances of the films' manufacture. This goes far beyond picturing the various 'authors'. These sequences also invoke and augment a wholly different fictive realm: the popular imagination of 'Tinseltown', with its own cast of heroes, villains, and clowns.

In most cases, there is also another point of difference. Whereas caricatures of actors are designed to be readily identifiable to general audiences, the same can seldom be said for the crew—rendering them in-jokes accessible to relatively few. Thus, while crew caricatures can occasionally be found, such as producer Harriet Parsons and director George Marshall in *Never a Dull Moment* (1950), it is far more common to find cartoons embodying clichés of a particular job role than the likeness of a specific individual. As Mallory Andrews notes of Sam Berman's designs for *Nothing Sacred*, these are "likely artist's renditions rather than straight caricatures as evidenced by

Nothing Sacred (1937)

the credit for composer Oscar Levant, whose bespectacled cartoon counterpart looks nothing like his distinctive hang-dog face."[5]

Title sequences of this ilk poke fun at the credited crew and, more significantly, at the wider roles and Taylorised 'film factory' institution they represent. They also illustrate two interrelated assumptions on the part of the title designers. One is that audiences already have some familiarity with popular discourses surrounding film production. The other is that they will 'get the joke' and will find these send-ups of the crew comical, pleasurable, and an enhancement of the overall viewing experience— despite their having, frankly, very little to do with the content of the 'main text'.

While the representations of some roles are limited to pretty basic associations (a man with a movie camera for the cinematographer; a man or woman with a tailor's dummy for the costume designer) others include flourishes indicating an imagined artistic temperament. For instance, the art director of *Nothing Sacred* is characterised as a French artist, sporting a beret and brandishing an enormous dripping paintbrush (although art director Lyle Wheeler was certainly not French). Screenwriters tend to be shown frenetically inking reams of paper—be it with a typewriter, as in *It Ain't Hay* (Erle C. Kenton, 1943), or an oversized quill pen, as in *Block-Heads*. Credits for the music department regularly feature conductors and/or performers—not always in kindly ways. Class conflict is proposed in *It Ain't Hay*, which juxtaposes a conductor with a bow tie and a huge brush of upended hair with a bumpkin wringing musical notes from a broom. In even less generous fashion, *Road to Rio* imagines songwriters Johnny Burke and James Van Heusen as an organ grinder and his monkey. More tendentious humour can be seen in the film editor credits for *Block-Heads* and *Nothing Sacred* which show, respectively, a man with a huge pair of shears and a butcher with a hatchet.

Producer and director credits are especially interesting as each role has two conflicting sets of representations, with their interplay suggesting the dominance of the producer in some films and the director in others. Producers can be characterised as lazy and useless, or as aggressively hands-on. In *Block-Heads* the producer reads a newspaper at his empty desk, in *Houseboat* (Melville Shavelson, 1958) he reposes with his feet on the desk, and in *It Ain't Hay* he relaxes on a chaise longue. Conversely, in *Abbott and Costello in the Foreign Legion* (Charles Lamont, 1950) he pounds his head in frustration as he observes the slow progress made by the stars, and in *Road to Rio* he holds a sweating, quivering director by the ear.

The director, who is frequently identified by his megaphone and chair, is shown in several films as the intimidated lackey of the producer, or generally struggling to cope. In *Bell, Book and Candle* (Richard Quine, 1958), where cast and crew are represented by photographed tribal masks and figurines, the statue symbolising the producer is large and wields an axe while the adjacent director statue is tiny and squat. In *Never a Dull Moment* the producer (pictured as a piano player) remains cool and collected while the dishevelled director is knocked off his feet by a laughing horse. By contrast, *Houseboat*, *Two Girls and a Sailor* (Richard Thorpe, 1944), and *Mardi Gras* (Edmund Goulding, 1958) all picture the director as a circus ringmaster, cracking his whip and in overall control. Their variations notwithstanding, all these title sequences reinforce popular ideas about individual crew roles as well as notions of the inter-crew dynamics underlying the film production process.

Never a Dull Moment (1950)

CONCLUSION

Opening title sequences invariably reference elements extrinsic to the diegetic world they introduce; the presence of the credit titles means they cannot do otherwise. In the process, they invoke a wide range of other paratexts associated with star image, popular narratives and genres, and even the film-industrial institution at large. Although the sequences I discuss here constitute a small and distinct group (atypical in its inclusion of cartoons or caricatures) they offer a clear illustration of the wider ways in which the film viewing experience entails a dialogue between diegetic elements and non-diegetic reference points.

As peritexts, physically attached to the main filmstrip and experienced in direct continuity with subsequent frames, title sequences might be regarded as more closely linked to their 'main texts' than some other kinds of paratext. Yet, as Jonathan Gray has astutely emphasised, no paratext is "versus the text because it is part of the text".[6] All are constituent parts of the same sprawling mass of knowledge and experience. These title sequences are therefore representative of broader phenomena, setting an appropriate tone and encouraging a realistic set of expectations for the film at hand while also reinforcing the film-viewing dynamic as the act of consuming a manufactured entertainment product.

NOTES

1. Gerard Genette, *Paratexts: Thresholds of Interpretation* (Cambridge: Cambridge University Press, 1997), 1, 24.
2. Jonathan Gray, *Show Sold Separately: Promos, Spoilers, and Other Media Paratexts* (New York: New York University Press, 2010), 23.
3. Deborah Allison, "Beyond Saul Bass: A Century of American Film Title Sequences", *Film International*, 30 January 2011, http://filmint.nu/?p=202.
4. Trav S.D., "On the Important Cultural Role Played by W. C. Frito", *Travalanche* (blog), 29 January 2015, https://travsd.wordpress.com/2015/01/29/on-the-important-cultural-role-played-by-w-c-frito.
5. Mallory Andrews, "*Nothing Sacred* (1937)", *Art of the Title*, 18 July 2017, www.artofthetitle.com/title/nothing-sacred.
6. Robert Brookey and Jonathan Gray, "'Not Merely Para': Continuing Steps in Paratextual Research", *Critical Studies in Media Communication*, vol. 34, no. 2 (2017), 102.

First published in *Film International*, issue 91, vol. 18, no. 1 (2020), 82–88. DOI: 10.1386/fint_00010_1.

TITLE SEQUENCES IN THE WESTERN GENRE: THE ICONOGRAPHY OF ACTION

What role do opening title sequences play in shaping a viewer's experience of the coming film? The majority do a great deal more than simply name the picture and list the main credits. Indeed, the most intriguing thing about these sequences is that, for many viewers and designers alike, their most important functions often lie elsewhere.

In most pictures, filmmakers have made a double use of the time in which the credits run. For more than sixty years it has been extremely rare to find a feature film that does not follow this convention. On the one hand, filmmakers have honoured their contractual obligations to credit the contributions of cast and crew. On the other, they have employed various elements of image and sound in order to orient the viewer and to generate a range of expectations. These pointers partake in the process of transporting the viewer's consciousness out of the real world and into the world of the film. The techniques by which they have done so vary greatly. In some films, title sequence design closely maps the style of the coming film. In others, we find devices that would seldom be deemed appropriate elsewhere in most mainstream films (of the classical era, at least). The reason for the acceptability of elements such as still pictures, animation, and non-diegetic songs during the title sequence would seem to derive from their conjunction with the credit titles. These address the audience directly. Moreover, they invariably refer to elements outside the individual film, as well as within it. These factors delay the moment at which viewers can effect a psychological passage into the diegetic world, unhampered by overt narrational marks. Opening titles thus occupy a unique transitional zone that mediates between the main film narrative and the filmmakers' salesmanship of the motion picture to its audiences.

The purpose of this paper is to explore some of the ways that analysing opening titles can help us to understand the processes by which filmmakers forge an implicit contract with their audiences. In order to do so, it makes use of a detailed case study of title sequences in the Western genre. The findings presented arise from a stratified random sample of the opening title sequences of 2,636 American feature films of the sound era, of which 270 are Westerns. From this survey, a wide range of representative examples have been selected for discussion.

In particular, this study demonstrates the extent to which each of the films examined has used its opening title sequence in order to prepare the audience for the viewing experience ahead. Despite the enormous potential that title sequences offer for enhancing understanding of this process, they remain a shamefully underused resource in film studies. Whilst the literature on title sequences has grown considerably in recent years, this movement has occurred primarily within the field of graphic design rather than film academia. Consequently, appreciation of such issues as the relationship of title sequences to narrative, and the historical correlation between title design and film genre, are underdeveloped. The film studies discipline would benefit from creating its own literature on these topics in order to reach a greater understanding of the ways such processes operate.

GENRE AND INTERTEXTUALITY

"Genres do not consist solely of films", Steve Neale has argued. "They consist also of specific systems of expectation and hypothesis which spectators bring with them to the cinema and interact with the films themselves during the course of the viewing process."[1] By the time a viewer sits down to watch a motion picture, he or she will normally have been exposed to a wide range of materials that will have shaped in some way his or her expectations of the coming film. These will almost certainly include at least one of a range of publicity materials, such as posters, trailers, and print advertisements. All these materials are designed by the film's producer, distributor or, occasionally, its exhibitor, in order to encourage potential viewers to select and attend that picture. To this purpose, many of them emphasise the similarities between the new film and previous popular films. In making such connections, one of the most important frames of reference has always been genre. This tendency can be found across the full range of advertising media.

The very last piece of material that most viewers see before the main film begins will normally be its opening title sequence. It may rightly be argued that, unlike posters or trailers, say, the title sequence is an intrinsic element of the film itself. In many respects, though, it is also distinct and separate. The very fact that it has its own widely recognised designation is proof of this. In describing the position that title sequences occupy, Leo Charney has aptly drawn on Gerard Genette's writings on paratext. He shows how neatly title sequences fit Genette's classification of a domain that mediates between text and extratext; in this case, between the unique film that they belong to and the external features to which they point.[2] Title sequences thus help to shape audience expectations by invoking intertextual and extratextual features, as well as through their inclusion of elements specific to the film at hand. In order for this to occur, viewers must have some familiarity with relevant films, people or events that exist outside the diegetic space. This is likely to include a knowledge of the other work of personnel (stars, directors, etc.) who have worked on the project. As we shall see, generic recognition is a further ability that is often assumed.

Even the very name of a film often suggests its membership of a particular generic group. Westerns, perhaps more than any other genre, have tended to use extremely evocative titles. In the names of the films cited through the course of this paper, we find many examples of words and phrases that identify their membership of the genre. They do so in a range of ways. Some identify location, whilst other films are named after legendary figures or common character types. Many titles refer to objects or events that are totemic of life in the American West. Others cite specific incidents, either real or fictional. The name of the picture is arguably the most prominent and commanding link between the external publicity materials and the film itself. Its appearance on screen in the main title sequence is therefore loaded with the accumulated meanings born of all the other materials and discourses in which it has featured.

Whereas publicity materials such as trailers and magazine advertisements aim to influence audience purchase choices, by the time viewers see a picture's opening title sequence their decision has already been made. In consequence, the messages that title sequences send out are geared towards a slightly different objective. In short, the main title sequence should indicate the nature of the movie, anticipate its main pleasures and, through this process, it should help to ensure that the audience responds 'correctly'. That is, the audience should be encouraged to develop precisely the expectations that the film is able to satisfy.

Title Sequences and Westerns

In surveying the opening title sequences of a range of Western movies, it quickly becomes apparent that most of them make extensive use of intertextual references. This role is fulfilled not only by the credit titles themselves but it also features conspicuously in other elements of their design. At the forefront of this tendency lies the flagrant and repeated incorporation of elements so emblematic of the genre that they have often participated in its very definition. Most of these features are readily apparent on a surface level. This is important, since their role is to function as pointers for the audience, helping them to select the appropriate schemata for the viewing experience ahead.

Title sequences normally combine three elements of design: the credit lettering, the background image, and the soundtrack. Each of these aspects has particular forms that are strongly associated with the Western. Each of them can play an important part in influencing a viewer's expectations. In the analysis below, I have chosen to focus on the background images that underlie the titles. This choice is not intended to denigrate the very substantial contributions the other elements can make. It arises purely from the fact that space does not allow a comprehensive account of all three. It is therefore worth prefacing this analysis with a few words about credit lettering and soundtracks in Western films.

It has often been observed that the genre has long favoured a very distinctive style of credit lettering. In general terms, this is a fat face style with exaggerated slab serifs. Its most well-known variant is the popular 'Playbill' typeface. This was first developed in the 1860s and, as its name suggests, it was particularly associated with advertising posters. In many Western films it has been used diegetically, featuring on the familiar 'Wanted' posters, as well as in the title sequence. This is a clear example of the way that title sequences tend to reference distinctive elements of the film they introduce. In this case, the connotations of the typeface are so widespread that it has also acquired an intertextual and extratextual saliency. It has long been recognised as a powerful signifier of the Western genre (its occasional use elsewhere notwithstanding) and has been used in this way across a range of media, including films, books, and Wild West shows. Representative examples of its use in film title sequences can be found in *Wagon Master* (John Ford, 1950), *Rage at Dawn* (Tim Whelan, 1955), and *Cat Ballou* (Elliot Silverstein, 1965).

Westerns also have strong associations with particular musical styles. In most cases, the title sequence introduces one or more of the musical themes that will be found throughout the picture. Some sequences feature a more distinctive element however: a non-diegetic theme song. In Westerns, as in other genres, theme songs are less common than instrumental music. However, before their use was widely adopted in the 1960s, they were more common in Westerns than in any other dramatic

Wagon Master (1950)

genre. One reason for their popularity can be found in the drive to emulate the popular success of the theme song to *High Noon* (Fred Zinnemann, 1952).[3] Perhaps more important, though, is the role their lyrics play in generating narrative expectations.

Many Western theme songs describe characters and plot in a surprising level of detail, referencing archetypal generic scenarios in order to do so. The lyricist Ned Washington can be seen as a central figure in the refinement of this important narrational role. His work includes the theme songs for *High Noon, The Man from Laramie* (Anthony Mann, 1955), and *Gunfight at the OK Corral* (John Sturges, 1957). This narrational function was to become a generic convention in itself. As a body of work, Western theme songs play a central part in binding the individual films they introduce into the genre as a whole. Moreover, in citing key thematic and iconographic motifs they have augmented the prototype Western schema. Their succinct verbal articulation of character and narrative formula has made an important contribution to the genre's heritage.

CLASSIC FEATURES OF WESTERN TITLE SEQUENCES

A statistical comparison between Western title sequences and those of other genres reveals several differences in the relative popularity of different types of background image. Until the late 1950s, films were most likely to present their titles over one or more still pictures. As far back as the late 1940s, though, a gradual movement can be detected whereby, irrespective of their genre, films shifted towards the adoption of moving images and, later, narrative action. It is significant that Westerns were at the forefront of this movement. In particular, they began to introduce motion photography of action scenes with greater regularity than other genres. By the late 1940s (1945–49), over 38% of Westerns were already using action-based backgrounds. This seems a staggering proportion when one considers it in comparison with the mere 6.6% of other films that did so. This artistic choice is very significant. Its result is the immediate introduction of two of the genre's most essential features. Western movies almost invariably centre on action and movement. They also take place in a setting that has a very distinctive iconography. By establishing these features at the outset, title sequences whet the anticipation of central generic pleasures, directing audience expectations towards the entertainment experience the film will deliver.

In a review of *The Hi-Lo Country* (Stephen Frears, 1998), Ed Buscombe describes his impression of the archetypal Western title sequence. He outlines its "confident opening on a huge, flat landscape, followed by (as with all proper Westerns) a shot under the titles of a man riding toward the camera."[4] He is unlikely to be the only viewer holding an impression of this kind. The frequent repetition of styles and images has ensured the ubiquity of such ideas. Strongly developed associations between image and genre have both drawn on and contributed to their iconic power.

Buscombe's analysis pinpoints one of the genre's most pervading images, both within and without the title sequence. Its three elements—landscape, man and horse—feature regularly in opening titles, both separately and together. Landscapes are the most prevalent. They have been depicted using a range of techniques, including paintings, photographs, and motion photography. In some sequences they participate in an action scene, whilst in others they are the only pictorial element present. Given that the Western genre is defined by its setting as much as anything else, orienting the film is this way provides a fitting introduction. There is considerable variation in the nature of the landscapes depicted. Indeed, contrary to Buscombe's claim, mountainous terrain is especially common. Whatever the case, the landscape almost invariably displays the characteristics John G. Cawelti has isolated: "its openness, its aridity and general inhospitality to human life, its extremes of light and climate and, paradoxically, its grandeur and beauty".[5]

Rugged, inhospitable terrain can be seen in the title sequences of *The Cisco Kid and the Lady* (Herbert I. Leeds, 1939), *Riders of the Purple Sage* (James Tinling, 1941), *Mule Train* (John English, 1950), *Across the Wide Missouri* (William A. Wellman, 1951), and *On Top of Old Smoky* (George Archainbaud, 1953), to name but a few. A significant feature of this type of landscape is the extent to which it can be read as hostile and full of dangers. Such a setting is able to participate in the film's story instead of acting merely as a backdrop to it. The role of landscape in the Western genre is twofold. As well as indicating that the film takes place in the American West (and is thus entitled to generic membership) it adopts a narrative function whereby men battle against their environment. In landscape images we find one of the most profound expressions of the wilderness/civilisation antinomy that Jim Kitses, and other critics after him, have identified as one of the genre's most important themes.[6]

Whilst open landscapes feature most often, Western title sequences have sometimes promoted other iconic settings. The archetypal Western town can be seen in several films including *Yellow Sky* (William A. Wellman, 1948) and *A Lawless Street* (Joseph H. Lewis, 1955). The first of these uses a lithographed picture whilst the other presents a photographic image that erupts into action when a rider appears at the end of the sequence. While the similarities between these sequences signal their shared generic origin, their differences are tailored to features of the individual films. When the band of outlaw protagonists arrive in the eponymous Yellow Sky, they find that it is a ghost town. The lithographed title card freezes the town's image in history, just as it seems empty and petrified to the arriving refugees. *A Lawless Street*, on the other hand, quickly moves to show the situation that its title describes.

The sequences described above show only scenery but many other landscapes feature humans or their property. Where this occurs, Buscombe has rightly noted that a man on horseback is the most common image. Lest my subsequent account prompts accusations of sexist language, it should be noted that representations of women are extremely rare. They can be found only in such

Westerns as *Forty Guns* (Samuel Fuller, 1957) and *The Quick and the Dead* (Sam Raimi, 1995) that feature a female protagonist in a 'masculine' role.

The appearance of riders or other figures in the landscape increased as Western title sequences moved towards the widespread adoption of motion photography. This is unsurprising, since the incorporation of characters often represents the instigation of the narrative. Moreover, horsemen are intimately associated with the spectacle of movement, which is arguably the Western genre's most visceral pleasure. Even in title sequences based around paintings, such as *Knight of the Plains* (Sam Newfield, 1939) and *In Old Montana* (Raymond K. Johnson, 1939), we find that depictions of men on horseback are calculated to create the impression of movement. In one painting the horse rears on its hind legs, whilst the other presents a frozen moment of a horse galloping at speed.

Knight of the Plains (1939) and *In Old Montana* (1939)

The ways in which characters interact with the landscape can reveal a great deal about the ensuing film. Establishing this relationship during the opening titles indicates the extent to which they have control of the environment they occupy. Furthermore, a comparison of the title sequences of *The Westerner* (William Wyler,

1940) and *Shane* (George Stevens, 1953) illustrates an observation made by many analysts of classical cinema. This is that a film's beginning is often mirrored or repeated in its final frames; the opening images not only represent the film's start but also its end. In these pictures, each title sequence centres on a lone rider who occupies, at some stage, almost the full height of the frame. Both riders are framed amidst characteristic Western topography and both command their landscape, not the other way around. The landforms of *The Westerner* are very flat whilst the mountains and valley of *Shane* are so far below the rider that they seem to have been levelled out. These films take place mainly within a fixed locale. There is little sense of the dangerous travel that features in so many Western pictures. The hazards that these heroes must face lie elsewhere, in the other men that occupy or enter that territory.

The Westerner (1940) and *Shane* (1953)

In each sequence, the landscape composition emphasises the importance of the rider. In *The Westerner*, the low horizon line and convex curve of dark clouds above surround an area of brightness which forms the immediate background to the almost silhouetted figure. The gentle curves of the mountains and foliage in *Shane* form a similarly centrifugal ring around the centre of the frame into which the rider approaches. These devices confirm that the figures shown are those who are in some way named by the very title of each film. They signal that each man will play a central role in the narrative ahead. The main difference between the two images is that 'The Westerner' faces the camera whilst Shane looks away from it. This camera angle can be read as a sign of Shane's transience, prefiguring his departure at the end of the picture. He will remain an enigmatic wanderer who cannot be held by either the viewer or the characters in the film. The title design of *The Westerner* produces the opposite effect.

The relationship between men and landscape has often been expressed through shot scale. Very long shots are particularly prevalent and are normally used to emphasise the characters' vulnerability in a hostile terrain. The title sequence of *Winchester '73* (Anthony Mann, 1950) provides a good example. In an unbroken shot, a slow pan tracks the progress of two riders on the horizon line of a landscape of rolling hills. It is the first of many such shots which show the riders' arduous journey in search of the eponymous gun. The territory holds many hazards, such as warmongering Indians, and the opening shot is indicative of the protagonists' disadvantage in the open terrain. *The Last Sunset* (Robert Aldrich, 1961) also employs extremely long shots in its depiction of two riders crossing a range of hostile landscapes. Indeed, the figures of the riders here are so small that they would scarcely be visible were it not for the clouds of dust thrown up by the hooves of their galloping steeds. Their rate of progress emphasises the spectacle of movement, an effect intrinsic to the genre. *Duel at Diablo* (Ralph Nelson, 1966), which also tracks the course of a barely visible rider, makes particularly explicit the filmic attraction of the landscape itself: its stunning cinematography is coupled with a title announcing the shooting location. In the vastness of such terrains as these, the riders are shown to be both bold and vulnerable. Analysis of *The Stalking Moon* (Robert Mulligan, 1968) demonstrates that the size of a figure in the landscape does not necessarily bear a proportionate relationship to his power over it, however. In each shot, this man appears as a very tiny figure but, far from being overpowered by the rocky outcrops through which he picks his way, it is at his command. The protection that the landscape provides for the gunman means that he can participate in its latent menace.

Some of the most powerful and iconic images of men negotiating the barren Western landscape can be found in the films of John Ford. The opening titles of *Stagecoach* (1939), *Three Godfathers* (1948), *Fort Apache* (1948), *Wagon Master*, and *The Horse Soldiers* (1959) have much in common with one another. Each makes frequent use of long shots of silhouetted riders crossing desolate terrain, normally at a diagonal angle to the camera. These frame compositions are strongly consistent with images found later in the films. They are self-consciously artistic and have conspicuously higher production values than most other Westerns of the studio era. They consequently prefigure elements of Ford's individual directorial style as well as some of the most basic iconic elements of the genre and of the films' specific narratives. The travellers are normally identified as members of a particular social group, such as cavalry, Indians or migrants. This designation foreshadows the familiar narratives associated with these groups. For instance, the title sequence for *Stagecoach* includes representations of stagecoach travel as well as images of cavalry and Indians. The accompanying music—a medley like the images—adopts a more dramatic tone at the appearance of the Indians. It thereby reinforces the association between these images and anticipated narrative events.

The iconic images that Western title sequences present have often extended beyond characters and landscapes. The accoutrements that signal a protagonist's nature and his narrative role have often been highlighted. It has been shown that man is seldom seen without his horse. Another totemic item is his gun. The importance of this instrument has often been emphasised visually and it has also featured in the lyrics of a range of title songs, such as *Gunfight at the OK Corral* and *Captain Apache* (Alexander Singer, 1971).

The persona of the Western hero frequently finds expression in the equipment that he carries. *The Naked Spur* (Anthony Mann, 1953) is a case in point. It opens with the image of a mountainous landscape. To the accompaniment of dramatic music, a zip pan shifts the image to a riding boot adorned with a shining spur. A slower pan re-frames to show the entire horse and rider, whom it follows as they journey toward the distant horizon. Like *Shane* and *The Westerner*, this sequence forges an immediate link between the man depicted and the title of the film. It establishes that the rider is central to the narrative. It implies that the cruel spur defines his character and, furthermore, suggests that the spur will feature as a recurrent narrative motif.

The opening titles of *The Man from Colorado* (Henry Levin, 1948) establish characterisation without ever showing the eponymous hero. The sequence opens on a close-up of a holstered pistol. The first title card is revealed when a man's hand picks up the gun. Before he is even seen, the 'Man from Colorado' has already been identified as a gunman. As such, he can immediately be placed within a range of generic character types, and

The Lawless Breed (1952)

associated narratives are called to mind. Similarly, *The Lawless Breed* (Raoul Walsh, 1952) does not show any characters in its title sequence. Instead, a tabletop arrangement of a gun and a hand of playing cards, topped by the ace of spades, is all that is needed to introduce the 'lawless breed' on which the film will centre.

GENERIC SELF-CONSCIOUSNESS IN THE 1960S AND BEYOND

The opening titles analysed above span several decades but most were made between the 1930s and the early 1960s. Any later sequences discussed bore marked similarities to those of earlier years and tended to function in very similar ways. Each sequence reinforced general impressions of what defines a Western film. Many of them invoked generic knowledge in order to suggest the types of narratives which would follow. In each of them we can observe the filmmakers' consciousness of working within generic parameters. The title designs can also be seen to embody their assumption that audience members will be complicit in the process of consumption within these boundaries. Not all Western title sequences since 1960 bear such a straightforward relationship to the genre's heritage, however. Parody and pastiche are rife. As elsewhere, title design has continued to point up features of the coming film. The use of these techniques in opening titles from the late 1960s onwards can thus be seen as symptomatic of a more pervasive attitude toward the genre and its history.

The iconography of *The Great Train Robbery* (Edwin S. Porter, 1903), which is often cited as the first Western, has proved particularly appealing to generic revisionists. Its most famous shot showed an outlaw firing a gun towards the camera. Exhibitors were reportedly offered the option of showing it at either the beginning or the end of the film.[7] Its possibilities as a dramatic opening have naturally endeared it to the title designers of revisionist Westerns. Several of them have paid homage, including *100 Rifles* (Tom Gries, 1968), which recreated the image at the end of its title sequence, using it to separate the animated titles from the opening of the narrative.

Tombstone (George P. Cosmatos, 1993) went much further in signalling its relationship to this and other antecedents. The film opens with black and white archive footage. While this plays, the voice of the veteran Western actor Robert Mitchum sets the scene, introducing the figures of Wyatt Earp and Doc Holliday. The final grainy monochrome shot consists of the actual footage from *The Great Train Robbery* in which the outlaw fires at the camera. Whereas *100 Rifles* used this moment to mark the transition between the titles and the main action,

Tombstone uses it to mark the end of the pre-title exposition and to herald the main, and only, title. The opening titles of *Posse* (Mario Van Peebles, 1993) also drew on archive material. In doing so, they proposed a revision of traditional historical perspectives. The sequence employs faded photographs of black cowboys as preparatory evidence for the film's subsequent racial demythologising of the American West. Each title sequence suggests that, ideally, viewers should have sufficient knowledge of the genre's heritage to appreciate the extent of the films' revisionism.

Butch Cassidy and the Sundance Kid (George Roy Hill, 1969) also opens by quoting earlier traditions of representing the American West. In doing so, it points up the mythology that it will at once celebrate and strip bare. The whirr of a film projector is heard and an empty movie screen is shown at one side of the widescreen frame. In this screen-within-a-screen an intertitle appears, stating: "The Hole in the Wall Gang, led by Butch Cassidy and the Sundance Kid, are all dead now..." Flickering, sepia-tinted footage ensues, showing the gang holding up a train before riding off triumphantly. At the same time, the credits roll in the area of blackness at the opposite side of the frame. An iris out at the end of

Butch Cassidy and the Sundance Kid (1969)

the silent film is synchronised with the end of the credits. One final title follows, stating: "Most of what follows is true." The sequence shows some of the mythology associated with the American West. Furthermore, it indicates the considerable extent to which Western movies are responsible for generating it. The self-consciousness of the final title's direct address to the audience invites their complicity in continuing this process.

The use of recycled imagery is perhaps at its most blatant in *The Shootist* (Don Siegel, 1976). As the camera pans across a mountainous landscape, shown in sepia tint, dramatic music and the sound of gusting wind is heard. John Wayne's star credit precedes the main title after which a voiceover begins, accompanied by a montage of archive footage. The sequence edits together shots of a gun being fired and images of a progressively older John Wayne partaking in battles drawn from his earlier movies. "His name was J. B. Books and he had a matched pair of 45s with ivory grips that was something to behold", runs the voiceover. A biography and description of his character follows. The narrator continues, "He had a credo that went..." Wayne's own distinctive voice is now heard to declare, "I won't be wronged, I won't be insulted and I won't be laid a hand on. I don't do these things to other people and I require the same from them." The film returns to the original landscape shot and a figure can be made out approaching from the far distance. As he moves into a medium close-up, we see that it is a much older John Wayne.

There is never any question that this sequence introduces John Wayne, the star, as much as it does a diegetic character. In this tale of an ageing gunfighter, parallels between Wayne and his character J. B. Books are insistently drawn as, for instance, each battles terminal cancer. Wayne's last film is as much homage to his iconic star persona as it is to a tradition of Western movies. The title sequence serves to introduce the archetypal Western hero, as it does in so many other films of the genre, but this is not its only purpose. The pleasure of re-experiencing the clips of Wayne's earlier movies accords with the film's broader pleasures. It is impossible to view *The Shootist* without experiencing an acute awareness of both the cinematic and historical mythology that constitutes its heritage.

POINTING THE WAY FORWARD

Through the analysis of a range of Westerns, we have seen that title sequences of the genre are remarkably homogenous. The extent to which they vary from one another occurs within strict limitations and normally arises in response to significant features of individual film narratives. Barring the relatively rare cases when a plain background is used, Western title sequences generally include at least one iconic image. Landscapes are the most common of these. We also find regular depictions of the Western hero and of totemic objects which define his character and/or the coming conflicts in which he must prevail. The iconography of action, such as horses and guns, is often present. Indeed many Western films use action footage in the title sequence itself, adopting this technique years before it was accepted as common practice in other genres. In privileging such core generic features, opening title sequences invoke familiar formulas and arouse specific narrative expectations. These features have been repeated so often, in title sequences and elsewhere, that later revisionist films have found it easy to reference their legacy.

Aside from their early adoption of the motion photography of action scenes, Western title sequences show no large-scale structural divergences from those of other genres. Instead, the accumulation of many relatively minor features, such as lettering style, landscape and iconography, makes them recognisable as a body of work. Their use of one or more pertinent generic features helps them to point to the pleasures of the forthcoming genre film and to cue appropriate cognitive models. Looking at just a handful of Western title sequences allows the formation of a fairly encyclopaedic picture of the genre's main features. Although my account is based on the empirical study of a sample of films, it seems safe to assume that the majority of themes and structures I have isolated were put there quite deliberately by the filmmakers. They are not subtext. To say that such features as masculinity, guns, horses, and landscape are recurrent preoccupations adds nothing to what has already been said about the Western by critics and theorists, nor to the general viewer's appreciation of the form. These things are at the core of what defines Western movies. As such, they represent an explicit communication of formula between filmmakers and audiences.

It is perhaps less useful, therefore, to ask what we can learn about Westerns from their title sequences than to ask what we can learn about the functioning of title sequences by examining them within the context of genre study. The answer, quite simply, is that title sequences not only introduce the unique film, but they can also act as points of intertextual reference. Cross-referencing within the parameters of genre can be a very powerful tool in structuring the inception of the viewing experience. Most title sequences, irrespective of film genre, have one very important feature in common. This is an attempt to set the scene for the film and/or to create an appropriate tenor that will put the viewer in a frame of mind where he or she will be most receptive to the subsequent narrative.

Opening titles form a gateway into the experience of watching a movie and can play an important role in shaping the spectator's involvement with it. Indeed, it is high time for film studies to acknowledge that title sequences can be used not only as a gateway into individual films but also as a route to a further understanding of the ways in which filmmakers engage their audiences.

NOTES

1. Steve Neale, *Genre and Hollywood* (London: Routledge, 2000), 31.
2. Leopold Joseph Charney, *Just Beginnings: Film Studies, Close Analysis and the Viewer's Experience* (Ann Arbor: UMI, 1993), 43.
3. Deborah Allison, "Do Not Forsake Me: The Ballad of *High Noon* and the Rise of the Movie Theme Song", *Senses of Cinema* 28 (2003), https://www.sensesofcinema.com/2003/cinema-and-music/ballad_of_high_noon/.
4. Ed Buscombe, "*The Hi-Lo Country*", *Sight & Sound*, vol. 9, no. 8, August 1999, 45.
5. John G. Cawelti, *The Six-Gun Mystique*, Second Edition (Bowling Green: Bowling Green State University Popular Press, 1984), 67.
6. Jim Kitses, *Horizons West* (London: Thames and Hudson, 1969), 11.
7. Barry Salt, *Film Style and Technology: History and Analysis*, Second Edition (London: Starword, 1992), 54.

First published in *Quarterly Review of Film and Video*, vol. 25, no. 2, March 2008, 107–15. DOI: 10.1080/10509200601074611.

DO NOT FORSAKE ME: THE BALLAD OF HIGH NOON AND THE RISE OF THE MOVIE THEME SONG

'Do Not Forsake Me', or 'The Ballad of High Noon', is perhaps one of the most widely known and fondly re- membered theme songs of all time. Its colossal success depends on far more than a catchy tune though. The ways that it was used within as well as without the film *High Noon* (Fred Zinnemann, 1952) were extremely pro- gressive. It was tremendously influential and, as I will show, helped to popularise the use of theme songs in later years as well as to define the lyrical style that would dominate title songs in Western movies. It was also immensely effective in the way that it guided viewers' expectations of the film, helping to shape their experience of it. For fans of the Western genre it is an especially in- teresting work as its lyrics lay bare some of the genre's most central features, as well the issues and concerns central to the film at hand.

In 1952, when *High Noon* was released, few dramatic films featured songs. Where they did exist, they were mostly diegetic. The decision to open the film with a song that functions so overtly as a narrational device is consequently striking and its implications are diverse. They can, for the most part, be placed within two categories however: one of these is narration and the other is marketing.

High Noon was by no means the first film to be cross-marketed with a song or musical score. Although the first film soundtrack album, *The Jungle Book*, was not released until 1942, merchandising of film songs either as short play records or sheet music had already been common practice for some years.[1] In August 1929, the *New York Times* was quick to report:

> Boundless radio has found a common denominator with the audible cinema, the theme song; and already *The Pagan Love Song*, *Evangeline*, *Broadway Melody* and *The Breakaway* are persisting through the tubes.[2]

The author of this article notes that as early as the late 1910s theme songs proliferated in 'silent' cinema, both as live accompaniment to film screenings and in other arenas of circulation, and cites the theme songs for *Mickey* (Richard Jones, 1918) and *The Bluebird* (Maurice Tourneur, 1918) as early examples. Russell Sanjek argues that *Mickey* was responsible for demonstrating to the film industry how valuable a popular song could be for promoting a film.[3]

This lesson was repeated many years later when *High Noon* set a new standard for effective cross-promotion, and in so doing encouraged a horde of imitators. It won the Academy Award for Best Song and, according to Jonathan Groucutt, "opened the floodgates" for theme songs, initiating the "'hit-theme' mania" that had emerged in American cinema by the 1960s.[4] After the success of 'Do Not Forsake Me', there was a vast increase in the number of films, especially dramatic films, to open with a theme song during the credits. Between 1950 and 1954, only 13% of American feature films used this device. Over the next five years the percentage grew to 22% and by the late 1960s this figure had risen still further to 29%.[5]

The biggest rise in the use of theme songs took place within the Western genre, argues Ed Buscombe, who claims that after 1952 most major Westerns opened with a theme song. He observes that this trend also resurrected the career of ex-singing-cowboy star, Tex Ritter, performer of 'Do Not Forsake Me', who found new success as a vocalist for a number of Western movie theme songs in the 1950s.[6] As one 1953 newspaper journalist opined,

> Already the cycle is nobly launched, and judging from the rush around movietown to sign cowboy warblers who can give a pretty good imitation of Tex Ritter's agonised delivery of Gary Cooper's musical woes in *High Noon*, any picture of the Old West without such accompaniment may go begging for theatre engagements.[7]

If the escalating popularity of theme songs can be partly explained by the success of *High Noon*, it should nevertheless be recognised that wider industrial factors underlay this trend. The drive to release theme songs through newly acquired or created recording arms of film companies had been hastened by the divorcement decrees of 1948. The severance of exhibition outlets from production companies and the loss of guaranteed revenue that these anti-monopolistic mandates caused, led production companies to seek alternate channels of gain. One of these was the expansion of their recording arms, and a more methodical cross-marketing of music and

High Noon (1952): British sheet music

film.[8] In 1951, a year before *High Noon*'s release, a record executive argued that, "A film company *must* have a record arm. It could lose money, and it would still come out way ahead on the promotion of basic product."[9] Jeff

Smith describes the way this sensibility influenced the release of *High Noon*:

> UA touted the *High Noon* campaign as one of the biggest ever, and it features many of the components that were commonly used in later promotions, such as multiple theme recordings and co-ordinated radio exploitation. [...] The centrepiece of the campaign was the six single releases of the film's theme song. Frankie Laine and Tex Ritter's versions, for Columbia and Decca respectively, were clearly the most important, but the tune was also recorded by Billy Keith, Lita Rose, Bill Hayes, and Fred Waring. [...] Whereas a record promoter would seek out sales and exposure of a particular version of the theme, UA simply sought as much repetition of the tune as possible.[10]

High Noon has acquired a reputation for precipitating changes in the style of film scores more generally, as well as the ways in which they were marketed. Although 'Do Not Forsake Me' has, in itself, attracted considerable praise, the implications for later film music have been framed negatively by a number of musicians and critics. Some have argued that the desire to incorporate a theme that could be independently marketed took priority over the scoring of music appropriate to the film's narrative and mood. Composer Elmer Bernstein claimed that 'Do Not Forsake Me' precipitated the demise of the classical film score, whilst film historian Roy M. Prendergast went so far as to argue that it "unknowingly rang the death knell for intelligent use of music in films".[11] Dorothy Horstman blamed *High Noon* for killing off another musical genre, the cowboy song, as the "adult Western" took precedence over singing Westerns.[12] These criticisms may indeed hold some water but, at the same time, *High Noon* represented a renaissance in the way that title songs were adapted to narrational purposes, using 'Do Not Forsake Me' at the start of the film to lay out some of its central themes in a sophisticated fashion.

Before looking in some detail at the words of 'Do Not Forsake Me', and considering how the song relates to *High Noon*, as well as its relationship to the Western genre more generally, it is worth noting that the lyrics of different versions vary substantially from one another. Like several other movie theme songs of the 1950s, such as those of *The Man from Laramie* (Anthony Mann, 1955) and *3:10 to Yuma* (Delmer Daves, 1957), the version played in the film contains very specific narrative references that were toned down or removed in order to create a more universal tale for the release of tie-in singles. The lyrics of Frankie Laine's hit recording of 'Do Not Forsake Me' were thus amended to omit all direct references to the film's villain, Frank Miller (Ian MacDonald).[13] Ned Washington wrote the lyrics for all three of these songs and thus stands out as a figure of central importance in the development of the Western theme song during the 1950s. Generating a prolific quantity of similar material throughout this decade, which also notably included *Gunfight at the OK Corral* (John Sturges, 1957), he played a central role in securing the success of 'Do Not Forsake Me''s formula.

The most exceptional feature of the lyrics to the version of 'Do Not Forsake Me' that opens *High Noon* is the extent to which it summarises the plot, even suggesting the way in which the story ends. Narrative précis, as well as invocation of specific characters and narrative events, emerged as a fully fledged song genre in 1952. Several months before the release of *High Noon* another Western, *Rancho Notorious* (Fritz Lang, 1952), used a similar musical technique, although neither the film nor its theme song, 'The Legend of Chuck-a-Luck', ever achieved the same degree of fame or influence.

Perhaps the paradigmatic example of the Western theme song, 'Do Not Forsake Me' outlines the main story elements, including the initiating events, the backstory, and the primary conflicts that must be played out at the film's climax. Nevertheless, the strategy allows the preservation of a remarkable level of suspense. We know what the conflicts are that will be acted out, but not the details of their development.

High Noon is built around the taut anticipation of the arrival of the nefarious Frank Miller on the noonday train. The song develops the implications of this event, hinting at the coming duel between Miller and Sheriff Will Kane (Gary Cooper)—"I must face that deadly killer"—as well as endowing Kane with an emotional depth

High Noon (1952)

that is less fully evident from his actions on screen. It bestows upon the film an ongoing psychological tension, heightening the drama of each minute—"Look at that big hand move along, nearin' high noon"—as well as pointing forward to the climax.

The inevitable mortal battle with Frank Miller, indicated in the song, is the physical conflict that will provide the action and spectacle intrinsic to the genre. However, from our knowledge of the archetypal persona of the Western hero, coupled with Gary Cooper's star image, we can surmise that "torn 'twixt love and duty" provides the internal conflict that will be the film's driving force. Instrumental phrases from the song are used throughout the film and these persistently remind the viewer of the corresponding lyrics. Graham Fuller writes that, "with its throbbing tune and recurring line of desperation— 'what will I do if you leave me?'—[...] it provides a chilling motif, ebbing away at moments of despair to suggest the real reason for the torment etched on Kane's face".[14] At several points in the film, a line from the song is heard, complete with lyrics, but only very faintly. The technique is thus less intrusive than the verses that punctuate *Rancho Notorious* or *Gunfight at the OK Corral*, where fresh narrational commentary is added at each interjection.

At first glance the song seems very simple in both structure and message. A slightly closer look exposes a work of considerable complexity. Ostensibly addressed not to the viewer but rather to Kane's wife, Amy (Grace Kelly), the song jumps back and forth between tenses. It refers to historical events, such as the backstory of the conflict between Kane and Miller, and Miller's vow of revenge on Kane for putting him in jail: "He made a vow while in State's Prison, vow'd it would be my life or his". It also points forward to the choice that Kane will make when Miller arrives, born out of the emotional dilemmas that pervade the body of the film: "If I'm a man I must be brave". Its description of his predicament is centred on the choice he must make between "love and duty". This is a feature common to many Western films. Robert Warshow has argued that a general feature of gender relations in the Western is that

> If there is a woman [the hero] loves [...] he finds it impossible to explain to her that there is no point in being 'against' [killing and being killed]: they belong to his world. [...] In Western movies, men have the deeper wisdom and the women are children.[15]

In 'Do Not Forsake Me', as in 'OK Corral', the woman is invoked as support, a figure of strength in the background, without whom the hero cannot succeed. She is required to facilitate the hero's success in the physical realm by bolstering his psychological strength and yet, when it comes to a choice between honourable machismo and the love of a woman, she will almost inevitably lose out: "Although you're grievin', I can't be leavin' until I shoot Frank Miller dead."

Although the song lyrics are in the first person and seemingly derive from Kane, it is no secret that they are actually performed by Tex Ritter—his contribution is prominently advertised during the opening credits. Although this establishes a distance between these words and the character of Kane, who is not in any case a character we might expect to express himself in song, the technique is significantly different from the introduction to *Rancho Notorious* by an omniscient narrator who withholds information. 'Do Not Forsake Me' does not narrate with the benefit of hindsight, and yet the archetypal plot elements it invokes allow the viewer to extrapolate further narrative events, including the final showdown. The song appeals to our knowledge of other Western movies and in doing so it encourages us to model our expectations of the film according to generic conventions.

To précis the plot in the opening theme song may seem a curious ploy. One possible explanation of this strategy can be found in Richard Combs' identification of *High Noon* as representing a precise stage in the maturation of the Western genre. He argues that, "A developing sense of its own ritual is one of the things that defines the 'classic' Western, but also leads it to outstrip itself (as perhaps all classicisms must), and finally to dissolve itself".[16] Combs' observations of the ways in which the film schematically draws attention to its formal attributes are astute. Claude Mauriac's interpretation of the pleasures that we seek in watching this genre is perhaps more satisfactory however: "We love Westerns in proportion to whether they offer us just enough surprises to make us experience the pleasure of seeing images we have seen a hundred times before."[17]

In its avowal of the primary pleasures we derive from watching Western movies, and its meaningful augment-ation of the experience of viewing *High Noon*, 'Do Not Forsake Me' has secured for itself a prominent place in the pantheon of movie theme songs. The enormous cont-ribution it has made to the heritage of Western theme songs as well as the developing art of cross-promotional marketing deserve to be remembered in the present era where such synergy has come to be taken for granted. Through its narration of universal themes within a specific tale it is a unique piece of writing that has had everlasting repercussions.

NOTES

1. Jeff Rovin, *The Signet Book of Movie Lists* (New York: NEL, 1979).

2. New York Times, "Those Theme Songs!", *New York Times*, 4 August 1929, A5.
3. Russell Sanjek, *American Popular Music and its Business: The First Four Hundred Years—Volume III: From 1900–1984* (Oxford: Oxford University Press, 1988), 47.
4. Jonathan Groucutt, "Scoring for the Sixties", *The Movie*, vol. 7, chapter 75, 1498–1500.
5. Statistics given in this article are based on my survey of 2636 title sequences from American feature films of the sound period.
6. Ed Buscombe (ed.), *BFI Companion to the Western* (London: BFI/Andre Deutsch, 1991), 194.
7. Harold Heffernan, "The Minstrel is the Man of the Hour", *Baltimore Sun*, 26 July 1953, cited in Texas Jim Cooper, "Tex Ritter: His Songs and Personality Expressed the Ethos of our West", *Films in Review*, vol. 24, no. 4, April 1970, 211.
8. A detailed account of the film industry's move towards diversification and conglomeration, and the resultant increase in cross-promotion of films and records can be found in Jeff Smith, *The Sounds of Commerce: Marketing Popular Film Music* (New York: Columbia University Press, 1998). See also Alexander Doty, "Music Sells Movies: (Re)new(ed) Conservatism in Film Marketing", *Wide Angle*, vol. 10, no. 2 (1988), 70–79.
9. Cited in Smith, *Sounds of Commerce*, 59.
10. Smith, *Sounds of Commerce*, 59–60.
11. Russell Lack, *Twenty Four Frames Under: A Buried History of Film Music* (London: Quartet Books, 1997), 207; Roy M. Prendergast, *Film Music: A Neglected Art* (New York: W. W. Norton, 1977), 102–03.
12. Dorothy Horstman, *Sing Your Heart Out, Country Boy* (Nashville: Country Music Foundation Press, 1975, 1996), 331.
13. The Frankie Laine recording of 'Do Not Forsake Me' differs from the movie version in the first and third lines of the second verse—"I do not know what fate awaits me […] And I must face a man who hates me" replaces "The

noonday train will bring Frank Miller [...] And I must face that deadly killer"—and in the second, fourth, and fifth lines of the final verse—"You made that promise as a bride [...] Although you're grievin', don't think of leavin' now that I need you by my side" replaces "You made that promise when we wed [...] Although you're grievin', I can't be leavin' until I shoot Frank Miller dead."

14. Graham Fuller, "*High Noon*", *The Movie*, vol. 5, chapter 53, 1052–53.
15. Robert Warshow, "Movie Chronicle: The Westerner", in Gerald Mast and Marshall Cohen (eds.), *Film Theory and Criticism* (New York: Oxford University Press, 1974), 403.
16. Richard Combs, "*High Noon*", *Monthly Film Bulletin*, vol. 53, no. 629, June 1986, 187.
17. Cited in Lotte H. Eisner, *Fritz Lang* (London: Secker and Warburg, 1976), 301.

First published in *Senses of Cinema*, issue 28, September–October 2003. https://www.sensesofcinema.com/2003/cinema-and-music/ballad_of_high_noon/.

FILM TITLE SEQUENCES AND WIDESCREEN AESTHETICS

Filmed in black and white and framed in academy ratio (1.33:1), tuxedo-clad actor Tom Ewell approaches the camera, accompanied by the drone of an orchestra tuning up. "Ladies and gentlemen", he begins, as he introduces *The Girl Can't Help It* (Frank Tashlin, 1956). "This motion picture was photographed in the grandeur of Cinema-Scope and... pardon me..." With a quiet interjection of annoyance, he looks to screen left, takes a step toward it, and clicks his fingers. As if in response, the outer margin of the image recedes with a grating noise to present a wider view of the stage on which he stands. He walks to screen right, clicks his fingers again, and the screen expands to full CinemaScope dimensions. "As I was saying, this motion picture was produced in the grandeur of CinemaScope and in gorgeous lifelike colour by Deluxe." He pauses, looks up to the heavens, and repeats this phrase loudly, upon which colour leaches into the image. "Sometimes you wonder who's minding the store..." he complains disparagingly.

Significant industrial changes within the American film

industry, whether economic, technological, or both, have always resulted in attendant aesthetic upheavals. Film title sequences (and pre-title sequences, such as the above) provide a fascinating case study of the adaptation of film aesthetics and rhetoric in response to technological innovation. As we shall see, the ways in which the design of widescreen title sequences developed through the course of the 1950s and 1960s bore certain parallels to the evolution of widescreen filmmaking at large. After all, one of the longstanding purposes of opening title sequences has been to whet audience appetite for the film they are about to experience and to ensure their expectations are closely enough aligned with what the film will deliver to produce a reasonable chance of those expectations being satisfied.

Important differences exist nonetheless. Title sequences have always been set apart from the films they introduce. The very presence of the credit titles, which point to extratextual and intertextual elements, marks them off from the main body of the film. The incapacity for title sequences to present *only* a diegesis has legitimised the inclusion of a range of styles and techniques seldom to be found elsewhere in mainstream narrative filmmaking. As short pieces of film (a minority of which benefit from disproportionately high budgets and production values) they also provide an ideal test site for experimental film techniques. It is therefore unsurprising that many of these title sequences are forerunners of styles that came to be more widely adopted in mainstream cinema of later years.

The purpose of this essay is twofold. The first area I wish to explore is how, in responding to the advent of CinemaScope and other widescreen processes in the early-mid-1950s, title sequence designers sought to promote the advantages of these new formats to film audiences.

To this end, I pay particular attention to the prominent roles occupied by typographic shape, size, and layout in emphasising the new screen dimensions, as well as looking at some other devices used to trumpet what was clearly designed to be received and admired as a spectacular innovation. With film studios seeking to hammer home a consistent message, I also observe a tendency in title sequences of some early widescreen films to share a common rhetoric with their trailers and other advertising materials, although a detailed investigation of this phenomenon lies outside the scope of this essay.

My second (but by no means secondary) goal is to take a broader view of the changing aesthetics of film title design in widescreen cinema of the late 1950s and 1960s. Amid the various debates about the pros and cons of the wider aspect ratio for the cinematographic composition of live-action narrative content, we must recognise that this development impacted differently on the presentation of film credits. Title sequences pose a specific challenge quite distinct from those of the main body of the film: namely, the need to incorporate a lot of fragmentary written text.

Drawing mainly from my survey of title sequences in American cinema—while seeking the reader's forgiveness for throwing in a couple of irresistible examples from British films of the era—I show how the initial emphasis on the immersive magnitude of widescreen presentation began to be displaced by other graphic trends.[1] In doing so, I focus on the emergence of two new ways of balancing different elements within the frame. The first is asymmetrical frame compositions and the changing spatial relationships between main and credit titles and live-action footage; the second is more formal geometrical divisions of the frame and the use of split-screen and multi-frame effects.

Bigger and Better

The introduction and adoption of widescreen processes by the American film industry in the early 1950s was driven, as has been widely documented, by economic rather than aesthetic factors. Changing leisure habits (including, but not limited to, the rise of television ownership, which surged from 3.9 to 20.4 million households between 1950 and 1953) had contributed to plummeting cinema admissions.[2] The film industry had seen annual box office receipts slide year on year from an all-time high of $1,692 million in 1946 to just $1,187 million in 1953—an eye-watering 30% decline—and production companies were eager to find new ways to reverse the trend.[3] The strategy they hit upon was to make films "bigger and better", luring viewers back into movie theatres with the promise of an unrivalled entertainment experience that would be both spectacular and immersive.

The super-sized Cinerama format, which launched in 1952, proved too expensive and technically unwieldy to be rolled out across a significant number of cinemas (with a mere 22 capable of handling the format by 1959), but its popularity with audiences encouraged producers and exhibitors to adopt cheaper imitations.[4] At the forefront was CinemaScope, which was developed, heavily invested in, and aggressively marketed by Twentieth Century Fox from 1953 until it was superseded by other widescreen processes (most notably Panavision) in the early 1960s.

Although it was unusual for widescreen films to open with quite such a self-referential nod to their new technology and aesthetic as had *The Girl Can't Help It*, Hollywood studio executives, production personnel, and marketeers were all mindful of the commercial imperatives underlying the introduction of widescreen. John

Belton has likened Twentieth Century Fox's conversion to CinemaScope to "the grooming and packaging of a new star"—an analogy Keith M. Johnston also adopts in his analysis of trailers for early CinemaScope product.[5] The need to ensure cinemagoers were aware of, and suitably impressed by, the magnificence of what Fox liked to describe as a "modern miracle" would shape film content and marketing alike (see, for instance, the original theatrical trailers for *The Robe* (Henry Koster, 1953), *How to Marry a Millionaire* (Jean Negulesco, 1953), and *Beneath the 12-Mile Reef* (Robert D. Webb, 1953).

The opening titles of *The Robe*, the first CinemaScope film to be released, are designed to emphasise the spectacle of the new technology. Yet, as Belton observes, its purveyors sought to differentiate their product from its forerunner, the largely non-narrative Cinerama, and to define it according to a model "less that of the amusement park, which retained certain vulgar associations as a cheap form of mass entertainment, than that of the legitimate theatre".[6] To this end, the film opens with the Twentieth Century Fox and CinemaScope logos superimposed on a background of opulent red curtains. The title lettering appears in large gold capitals, after which the curtains open to reveal the first spectacular scene.

The Robe (1953)

The second CinemaScope release, *How to Marry a Millionaire*, starts in a similar fashion. Theatre curtains open to reveal a full orchestra, which plays a five-and-a-half-minute overture before the main titles begin over a sequence of background images of crumpled silks and jewellery items. The trailer had opened in just the same way, but went on to superimpose hyperbolic titles over the shot of the orchestra:

CinemaScope
The modern miracle
You see without special glasses!..
Brings you as our next attraction
An entire new world of entertainment
Never before possible
Now
To fill the CinemaScope screen
As only they can...
Comes an array of stars
As wonderful and exciting
As this great new motion picture miracle!

Whereas the trailer's condensed running time necessitated this superimposition, however, the feature film's uninterrupted overture emphasised more directly Cinema-Scope's aping of what James Spellerberg describes as "the aura of legitimate theatre: cultural superiority and patronage by a wealthy and sophisticated audience".[7]

The Walt Disney Company followed Twentieth Century Fox's example, and used theatre curtains as the backdrop to the title sequence for their own first CinemaScope film, *20,000 Leagues under the Sea* (Richard Fleischer, 1954), although they added a topical twist by projecting ripples of blue light across the velvet curtains. During the final credit, the curtains rise, but, rather than opening on a panoramic scene, they reveal a close-up of the book on which the film is based—another appeal to pre-approved quality, but a hackneyed device already familiar from countless academy-ratio literary adaptations.

While these early CinemaScope titles referenced theatrical traditions for a very specific purpose, they were far from the first films to use such devices. Among various earlier examples of title sequences revealed by the raising or opening of theatrical curtains are *A Double Life* (George Cukor, 1947), a drama in which an actor playing Othello takes his role a little too much to heart, and the musical comedy *Two Tickets to Broadway* (James V. Kern, 1951). Shots of orchestras had also been used before, but in *How to Marry a Millionaire* it is with very different effect from examples such as *Words and Music* (Norman Taurog, 1948) or *Unfaithfully Yours* (Preston Sturges, 1948). The first of these used editing to dissect the scene; the other employs a slow track in to the conductor's back. Neither sought to replicate the experience of sitting in a theatre.

Despite the presence of similar contrivances in later films, such as the theatrical biopics *Gypsy* (Mervyn Le Roy, 1962, filmed in Technirama) and *Star!* (Robert Wise, 1968, filmed in Todd-AO), there is little evidence that recourse to theatrical models became a significant element of widescreen titling. In *Gypsy* and *Star!* the choice doubtless owes as much to thematic appropriateness as to the general widescreen spectacle these films so successfully deliver. Instead, title designers of films following *The Robe* and *How to Marry a Millionaire* were largely preoccupied by other issues. Like the directors and cinematographers of widescreen movies, one of their main concerns was to find new ways of balancing visual elements in what many filmmakers and critics felt to be an impractically shaped frame.[8]

LETTERING SIZE AND EMPHASIS OF THE SCREEN DIMENSIONS

Among the extravagant claims made for CinemaScope in the theatrical trailer for *The Robe* was the proclamation that "you see more... because there is more of the film to see". Many widescreen title sequences were designed to emphasise the amplitude of the new frame dimensions, and often used the main title lettering as a tool for doing so. Yet lettering did not simply become larger, as one might expect. Even films such as *Bad Day at Black Rock* (John Sturges, 1955), *East of Eden* (Elia Kazan, 1955), and *Land of the Pharaohs* (Howard Hawks, 1955), which employed relatively large, heavy fonts for their main titles, tended to frame them comfortably with a generous margin between the text and the boundaries of the screen. We can observe, nevertheless, isolated examples of title sequences in which large lettering creatively showcases the dramatic possibilities of widescreen ratios.

Several films strive for this effect by creating the illusion of three-dimensionality. MGM's CinemaScope space opera *Forbidden Planet* (Fred M. Wilcox, 1956) uses a design in which the letters of the main title appear to be projected forward from a central point in the lower background of the screen space. Similarly, the main title

Forbidden Planet (1956)

of *South Pacific* (Joshua Logan, 1958, filmed in Todd-AO) blares out in exaggerated perspective upon back-thrusts emanating from a seascape's horizon line.

Both of these sequences (especially the earlier and arguably more effective opener for *Forbidden Planet*) adapt a technique that had been popularised by the short-lived technological rival CinemaScope had helped to vanquish: 3D cinema. Their resemblance to the in-your-face title sequences for such 3D films as *House of Wax* (André de Toth, 1953), *Invaders from Mars* (William Cameron Menzies, 1953), *It Came from Outer Space* (Jack Arnold, 1953), and *The Bounty Hunter* (André de Toth, 1954) is hard to miss.[9] By the time *Forbidden Planet* arrived on screens, it seems that CinemaScope was sufficiently well established that initial efforts to align the process with refinement and respectability were no longer considered necessary or relevant.

Other title sequences used lettering so large that even the expansive proportions of the widescreen frame could not contain it. An example of this effect can be seen in the Selznick Studio's lavish remake, *A Farewell to Arms* (Charles Vidor, 1957), in which the letters of the main title scroll from right to left across the screen. Here again, the technique was not in itself an innovation of widescreen cinema, having previously been used in a handful of epic, action-filled dramas including *Gone with the Wind* (Victor Fleming, 1939), *Boom Town* (Jack Conway, 1940), and *King Solomon's Mines* (Compton Bennett, 1950). Nevertheless, a visual rhetoric that equated the grandiosity of widescreen processes with that of their subject matter ("CinemaScope demands a bigger story, more action, whether outdoor or indoor or intimate", ran a 1953 trade ad) would find continued popularity in various forms.[10]

One sequence to do this particularly effectively is the

scaremongering nuclear-apocalypse drama *The World, the Flesh and the Devil* (Ranald MacDougall, 1959, Panavision), which opens with an image of a deserted metropolitan street, shown in exaggerated perspective. The main title appears in three sequential parts, each of which emerges from the vanishing point and increases in size as if it were advancing down the street towards the camera, before enveloping and finally disappearing 'behind' the camera/spectator. The significant difference between this sequence and *A Farewell to Arms* is its combination of width and illusory scenic depth. Together, these feign Cinerama's technique of drawing the viewer into the frame. This further illustrates the observation I made in relation to *Forbidden Planet* and *South Pacific*: that with the rollout of a plethora of widescreen processes in its advanced stages, the sideshow aesthetic so studiously avoided in early CinemaScope films became a legitimate means of presentation.

The examples I have given so far all centre on the substantial or illusory magnitude of the main title lettering. They do not, however, illustrate the full range of techniques designers have used to impress upon cinema audiences that, thanks to widescreen cinematography and projection, "there is more of the film to see". In some other cases, title designers employed lettering that was unusually small in relation to the overall size of the image. One example is *The Big Country* (William Wyler, 1958, Technirama), in which the smallness of most of the credits showcases the vastness of the wilderness landscape, contrasting its scope with the vulnerability and relative insignificance of the stagecoach travellers that cross it. Another is *The Greatest Story Ever Told* (George Stevens, 1965, Ultra Panavision 70), where, once again, the diminutive lettering instils a sense of grandeur and esteem to the whole. It involves an excruciatingly slow title crawl on a plain orange background and accompanied by church organ music. Lasting for a full three-and-a-half minutes, it is followed by an equally unhurried fifteen-second fade out. The film is, writes Derek Elley, "structured like a majestic symphony with Christ as the prime mover and central focus in a devout, almost funereal atmosphere".[11] Its title sequence radiates pomp and self-importance, reinforcing the message of the film title itself, which is that audience members should prepare to be awed.

There would seem, then, to be no hard and fast rules about the precise ways in which the advent of widescreen ratios affected the size of the title lettering. What does seem to be a common feature of many widescreen title sequences, especially in their first few years, is an attention to the relationship between the lettering dimensions and the proportions of the frame. In some of the examples we have considered, this extends to attempts to instil in their viewers a sympathy to the dramatic tonalities of the films' broader rhetoric.

ASYMMETRICAL FRAME COMPOSITIONS

The impact of widescreen formats on title design was far more extensive than experimentation with lettering proportions. A more dramatic and pervasive change in film titling aesthetics hinged on the horizontal positioning of main titles and credits. Prior to the arrival of Cinema-Scope, titles were almost always framed centrally, with asymmetric arrangements found only in the rarest of cases—such as *The Little Minister* (Richard Wallace, 1934), in which star credits were positioned next to framed photographs of the actors. From 1954 onwards, central justification of the credit titles quickly ceased to be the norm, and new ways of balancing them within the frame came into operation.

From the very earliest days of CinemaScope, designers began to experiment with new ways of positioning the credit titles. Most filmmakers clearly recognised that some care was required to present credits attractively and effectively—if one wished to avoid the kind of ugly jumble found in *Long John Silver* (Byron Haskin, 1954). A few, wedded to old habits, opted to stay within their comfort zone, subdividing the frame in order to arrange credits within a central area only minimally wider than the academy proportions they were used to. Thus, in *Demetrius and the Gladiators* (Delmer Daves, 1954) the edges of the frame are occupied by topical images of carved figural reliefs, which change with each title card but which always look towards the titles placed at the centre of the image. Similarly, in *The Black Shield of Falworth* (Rudolph Maté, 1954), titles are superimposed on a roughly 1.5:1-ratio heraldic wall-hanging, with a pair of statues filling the outer recesses of the screen, and in *Brigadoon* (Vincente Minnelli, 1954) the titles appear on an invitation card that lies atop a folded kilt.

In most cases, however, designers opted to modify traditional credit layouts in order to spread them across the width of the frame. These modifications were, in truth, quite minimal at first. One popular new convention, which arose very quickly, was to position star credits in horizontal rows of three, as illustrated in *Beneath the 12-Mile Reef*, *King of the Khyber Rifles* (Henry King, 1953), and *Garden of Evil* (Henry Hathaway, 1954)—a development that must have caused a fair few headaches for those tasked with negotiating star billing.

Although these early CinemaScope title sequences retained the tradition of symmetry, it was a convention that would soon begin to erode. The first significant landmark in the movement away from this aesthetic is arguably Saul Bass's design for the opening titles of *Carmen Jones* (Otto Preminger, 1954). This marked the art school-educated graphic designer's first foray into film title sequences—a field in which his modernist interventions would become enormously influential. The sequence featured an animated flame flickering in front of a stylised drawing of a rose, which remained at the centre of the frame, while the credit titles appeared sometimes in the middle, and at other times to one or other side of the frame. Bass's use of asymmetric credits would become a trademark feature of his work (regardless of aspect ratio) and was, like his other design innovations, much copied.

Yet there are also other reasons why decentralised frame compositions became normalised very quickly and were widely adopted from the mid-1950s onwards. Through the course of the late 1940s and 1950s, the average length of opening title sequences grew steadily, as the rise of the package-unit system and negotiations by increasingly powerful unions ensured more prominent (and spread out) credits for key production personnel. This, in turn, encouraged filmmakers to maximise the entertainment value of the time during which the credits ran. One effect of spreading out the titles, even if they remained centre-screen, was to reveal more of the background image. The introduction of widescreen processes allowed designers to capitalise further on this development and, by judicious placing of the credit titles, to give new prominence to other visual features.

In this way, a symbiotic relationship developed between titling and other components of the widescreen image. Increasingly, we can observe the filmmakers' efforts to arrange image and text in ways that are designed to complement one another; to ensure that credits are prominent and clearly legible while also endowing the imagery with a new importance. Countless examples can be found, irrespective of whether the sequence features paintings, drawings, photographs, animation, or live-action cinematography.

The opening title sequences of *Les Girls* (George Cukor, 1957, CinemaScope) and *Can-Can* (Walter Lang, 1960, Todd-AO) both feature a series of painted title cards in which the various elements of the image are arranged so that the full breadth of the screen is occupied by elements of visual interest. In each case, a slight asymmetrical bias allows credits, portraiture, and other representational images to command equal space and attention. In *Les Girls*, further visual interest is added by a series of elaborate shot transitions, including the rotation of a row of vertical slats, which capitalises further on the aesthetic possibilities offered by the wider frame.

Les Girls (1957)

Another tactic designers have used to achieve compositional balance is the placement of one or more titles at one side of the screen and a visual image in an approximately mirroring position at the other. One example is provided by the live-action title sequence for *Man of the West* (Anthony Mann, 1958, CinemaScope). The film begins with a centred production company credit over a panoramic shot of rugged mountain and desert terrain, before cutting to a closer angle as Gary Cooper's credit appears at screen left. A fraction of a second later, the star rides into view from off-screen right. He reins his horse in to a halt, and holds it in a position that occupies virtually the whole of the right half of the frame, remaining in this pose during the main title and the rest of the actor credits. A cut back to the first camera set-up shows him riding away towards the horizon, always keeping in the right half of the frame while the technical credits appear to the left.

In *Les Girls, Can-Can*, and *Man of the West*, the spatial relations between lettering and other imagery remains constant within each shot, in rather static and studied compositions. Yet, as filmmakers of the 1950s and 1960s responded to the contractual necessity of longer title sequences, a growing number introduced diegetic and, increasingly, narrative material. This called for a more complex relationship between the live-action photographic elements and the credit lettering.

In one masterfully choreographed sequence, titles are composed around static objects, which are discovered as a fluid camera roves around a shop retailing tribal art. The first shot of *Bell, Book and Candle* (Richard Quine, 1958, 1.85:1 ratio) shows Christmas shoppers in a snowy street. The camera tracks in towards the window of the store, before a cut repositions it inside. As the camera explores the wares, it periodically comes to rest on individual African masks, figurines, and fetishes. Each time the camera pauses, it does so in a way that frames the object off-centre, thus allowing titles to appear adjacently, rather than obscuring the object with superimposed text. Nor is this the only way in which the filmmakers arrange the titles and artefacts to complement one another. In one shot, we see five figurines grouped together

Bell, Book and Candle (1958)

on a shelf and accompanied by five actor credits, while the positioning of other credits humorously suggests parodic representations of the stars. Thus James Stewart's name appears next to a tall, skinny wooden figure; Kim Novak's is beside a beaten metal image of an elegant female face, and Jack Lemmon's accompanies a shrunken head. A further joke depicts the producer as an imposingly large figure, clutching an implement that might well be a weapon, after which the director is represented by a very tiny figure indeed. After the final credit, the camera tilts up to a live cat on a shelf, in a seamless transition from the wilfully self-reflexive title sequence to the internal coherence of the 'film proper'.

Sequences featuring live action, and especially those depicting characters and significant narrative incidents, tend to present the positioning of the titles as a more casual affair than in the instances described above, although such impressions are doubtless often illusory. For instance, *Written on the Wind* (Douglas Sirk, 1956, 2:1 aspect ratio) entails an elaborate choreography of titles, characters, and actions. It opens with one of the story's climactic scenes, as a drunken Kyle Hadley (Robert Stack) drives recklessly to the family mansion one night. Alerted by the noise, its inhabitants rise and come to their windows, with lead characters Marylee (Dorothy Malone), Lucy (Lauren Bacall), and Mitch (Rock Hudson) framed in turn next to their actor credits. Throughout the sequence, the credit lettering is positioned either to the left or right of any frame containing narrative content, so as to avoid obscuring moments of action.

As time went on, the narrative elements of live-action title sequences began to gain greater primacy. Thus, in films such as *Butterfield 8* (Daniel Mann, 1960, Panavision) and *Lonely are the Brave* (David Miller, 1962, Panavision), the placing of credits appears to be subordinate to a pre-existing choreography of action, rather than the two elements having been devised synergistically. In other words, the footage was probably shot without a detailed plan as to the precise placing of credits, which were subsequently superimposed in a way that would leave a fairly clear view of the characters at the same time as balancing the composition in a pleasing manner.

Decentralising the written text is one of the most enduring developments in the history of title sequence design. Although not all contemporary films use the technique, we have nonetheless come to accept decentralised titles as a standard feature in the majority of sequences that have anything else going on in the frame at all. Even as far back as the early 1960s, centralised titles were already starting to seem rather old hat in any aspect ratio. Yet, while the dominant trajectory was towards title sequences that sought to balance credit lettering with episodes of narrative action, the late 1950s and 1960s also saw a vogue for stylistic experimentation that took a very different route, and which gave rise to other kinds of widescreen composition.

GEOMETRICAL DIVISION OF THE SCREEN AND MULTI-FRAME EFFECTS

As we have seen, many widescreen films contrasted different types of visual content across the horizontal axis of the frame, or sought to arrange the various elements in mutually complementary ways. In other films, we can observe attempts to maintain audience interest in each part of the wider image by partitioning the frame into smaller sections. This is not at all the same as such early 'Scope films as *Demetrius and the Gladiators* or *The Black Shield of Falworth* that placed their titles in a central area and filled the sides of the image with thematically appropriate but entirely dispensable decorations. Even a sequence as simple as *I Married a Woman* (Hal Kanter, 1956, RKO-Scope), in which titles are placed to the right of boxed cartoon images of Diana Dors, assigns importance to the outer edges of the frame. Similarly, in *Kiss Them for Me* (Stanley Donen, 1957, CinemaScope), credits are arranged around a series of boxed images, which, in this case, vary in position so that the eye is drawn back and forth across the full breadth of the screen.

One thing they do indeed have in common with title sequences such as *Demetrius and the Gladiators* is that the screen space is treated as a flat canvas, with no real or illusory depth of field whatsoever. In many cases, the influence of magazine design and other two-dimensional graphic art is palpable. An early (and impure) example can be found in *Funny Face* (Stanley Donen, 1957, VistaVision), which opens in three dimensions, with a hand switching on a light box and placing onto it a transparency of Audrey Hepburn's face. It then proceeds to section later frames into flat, geometric areas in which there appear titles, photographs, and various ephemera associated with its fashion modelling story line. Indeed, this sequence was designed by the fashion photographer Richard Avedon, on whose life the film is loosely based.

The layout and use of space in Wayne Fitzgerald's title sequence for *Portrait in Black* (Michael Gordon, 1960, 1.85:1 ratio) also has strong stylistic echoes of 1950s magazine design. Though not set in the fashion world, the film's chic costumes and décor are clearly calculated to appeal to female viewers, and the stylistic similarity between its title design and women's magazines of the period is unlikely to be coincidental. It opens with the appearance of vertically animated coloured stripes to the right of an otherwise black frame. A photograph of Lana Turner replaces the stripes, switches from colour to black-and-white negative, and then moves across to screen left, where it is squeezed into a thinner strip. This process is repeated four more times, until negative images of all the main cast are lined up to the left of the frame with the main title to their right. The photographs switch back into colour, then negative again, and finally give way to coloured lines. The lines become animated, and part to form different groupings, among which the

Portrait in Black (1960)

remaining titles are staggered. Following this symbolic anticipation of the film's shifting character relationships, they all become strips of a single photograph, which is made whole at the end of the sequence when the masking (the space between the lines) disappears. A sophisticated appreciation of the possibilities of graphic layout is this sequence's most striking property.

Like *Portrait in Black*, many title sequences featuring geometric divisions of the frame do so in such a way as to accent the materiality of the image as a flat surface. *Silk Stockings* (Rouben Mamoulian, 1957, CinemaScope) animates rolls of variously coloured cloth, unfurling them across the screen, either horizontally or vertically, so that it is perpetually split into rectangles of ever-changing hues. During the main part of the title sequence for *Gay Purr-ee* (Abe Levitow, 1962, 1.85:1 ratio) the screen is split into numerous brightly coloured rectangles. The camera pans across the painted image, discovering credits and a few pictures drawn in spaces between the shapes. The sequence is reminiscent of Saul Bass's earlier design for *The Seven Year Itch* (Billy Wilder, 1955, CinemaScope), which also sectioned the frame into multicoloured rectangles, although in that case the overlapping shapes flapped open to reveal the credits—adding a modicum of depth to an otherwise flat plane.

The sequences described above are composed primarily of still pictures, abstract animation, or a combination of the two. Yet there are other sequences that section the frame into discreet areas, but which also incorporate live action or other motion footage. A rudimentary precursor can be found in *The Bonnie Parker Story* (William Witney, 1958, Superama), in which credits are superimposed on a brick wall to the left of a bedroom window through which we see a woman undressing. The effect, whether real or simulated, is that of a unified diegetic background, rather than a collage created during post-production, but, by the early 1960s, title sequences were using split-screen effects in a wide variety of ways— often assembling multiple segments of live action to run simultaneously.[12]

Like *The Girl Can't Help It*, *36 Hours* (George Seaton, 1964, Panavision) begins with a pre-title sequence in black-and-white academy ratio. It is comprised of news-reel footage depicting the manufacture of arms and the training of soldiers before the Second World War. This image moves across from its central location to the left side of the screen, and titles begin in white on a plain black background to the right. The titles and newsreel footage then alternate their positions for the remainder of the credits, after which the film switches to full colour. A variation on this design can be found in *Father Goose* (Ralph Nelson, 1964, 1.85:1 ratio), which opens with a full-frame image that shrinks to a fraction of its original size before, again, moving to one side when the credits begin outside of the live-action box.

36 Hours (1964)

Of course, not all title sequences using split-screen techniques positioned their credit titles outside the live-action window. This is particularly true of films using more than one segment of footage. A simple and effective example is provided by Maurice Binder's title design for *The Grass is Greener* (Stanley Donen, 1960, Technirama).[13] After an initial production company credit, a narrow slit of colour appears in the black background and widens to show a baby boy crawling on a grass lawn. The image width and content freeze when it has expanded to occupy 25% of the frame and the baby looks toward the camera. Cary Grant's credit appears superimposed on the tree canopy above the baby's head. A second window opens immediately to the right of the first, showing a baby girl on the grass. Deborah Kerr's credit follows within this window. A third opens to the extreme right of the screen. Robert Mitchum's credit appears, swiftly followed by another baby boy, who crawls into the image from beyond the margin of the frame. Each child looks to the screen left in turn, as the remaining black space at that side is filled with a fourth and final strip of footage containing another baby girl and Jean Simmons' credit. By this point, the screen space has been entirely filled, and split-screen imagery subsequently gives way to witty full-frame clips of babies playing with a typewriter, sheet music, a camera, and so forth, during the technical credits.

In the second half of the 1960s, other title designers went on to employ split-screen in even more elaborate and dynamic ways, often as elements in colourful and rapidly edited pop art montages. Indeed, such is their complexity, they are perhaps better described as instances of what Sergio Dias Branco has dubbed "the mosaic-screen", noting: "The split screen divides the screen into two or more parts. The mosaic-screen arranges one or more detached images on screen."[14] It is worth noting, moreover, that while the groundbreaking integration of multi-frame imagery in Saul Bass's acclaimed and influential title sequence for *Grand Prix* (John Frankenheimer, 1966, Super Panavision 70) would arguably have worked just as well in a narrower aspect ratio, many other sequences segmented the frame in ways that that would not have been possible in non-widescreen cinema.

The title sequence for the British spy thriller *Billion Dollar Brain* (Ken Russell, 1967, Panavision), another design by Maurice Binder, takes its inspiration from the eponymous mainframe computer, with its rows of buttons, whirring tapes and punch cards, and its ability to synthesise a large and complex array of data. These already repetitive visual elements are recombined in faster and faster multi-frame montages, until the screen is segmented into seven sections: three rectangular images to the top; three to the bottom; with the main title appearing in a thin horizontal strip between the two layers. "The split screen is routinely used to connect images whereas the mosaic-screen is habitually used to disconnect them", argues Branco, and this sequence certainly seems to put the onus on the viewer to re-synthesise the fragments— just as secret agent Harry Palmer (Michael Caine) must do with the help of the supercomputer.[15] Later frames, often featuring Caine alongside the genre-appropriate motifs of girls and guns, tend to be split vertically into three or more segments. At other moments, horizontal strips of masking in which further credits appear bisect otherwise full-frame imagery. Despite the varied and inventive visual permutations, one point of consistency throughout this sequence is Binder's maximisation of the possibilities offered by the Panavision ratio.

With the number of title sequences using multi-frame effects escalating in the late 1960s, the pinnacle of creativity was arguably reached in Pablo Ferro's 'mosaic-screen' contributions to *The Thomas Crown Affair* (Norman Jewison, 1968, 1.85:1 ratio). The elaborately

The Thomas Crown Affair (1968)

choreographed title sequence sometimes involves more than a dozen separate rectangles of imagery within a single frame. In some cases, fragments of a single picture are revealed in adjacent windows; in others, entirely separate images share a frame. Even where parts of a single picture appear simultaneously, varicoloured tinting almost always fragments it further. Although no live-action photography is used (except in the final moments), many of the images are mobile, gliding smoothly up, down, or across, behind the black masking in which the titles appear. Ferro's use of the widescreen space speaks loudly of his early employment as an artist at Atlas Comics, with the striking segmentation of the flat surface strongly reminiscent of comic book double spreads.

Although no other title sequences of the era matched the multi-frame intricacy of *The Thomas Crown Affair*, the trend for such mosaics continued. In *Marlowe* (Paul Bogart, 1969, 1.85:1 ratio), abstract lines shift to open a decagonal window to screen left, in which there appears a red-tinted image of a couple kissing by a pool. This remains on screen as the process is repeated to reveal an undercover photographer in a similar window to screen right. Later frames gain further interest from the designer's refusal to limit the mosaic fragments of imagery to the conventional squares and rectangles. Instead, frequent use is made of angular shards that rotate and close like the iris of a camera—drawing their motif from the activity of the eponymous private eye. And while the sequences described above separate their multiple images with areas of blackness, often containing credit titles, *The Trouble with Girls* (Peter Twekesbury, 1969, Panavision) goes a step further by placing windows of moving imagery within other images.

Split-screen and mosaic effects and other types of formal fragmentation of the widescreen image were nowhere near as widely adopted as the general shift towards asymmetrical titles and frame compositions, but they still participate significantly in wider aesthetic discourses. For one thing, they can be read as responses to early dialogues concerning the suitability of widescreen formats for the perpetuation of montage, deep focus, and other aspects of cinematic artistry.[16] While David Bordwell is essentially correct in his claim that "widescreen formats did not radically challenge, let alone overturn, classical Hollywood norms of shot composition", these title sequences do indeed present challenges to some of the norms that both predated and coexisted with them.[17]

As has often been the case, the paratextual nature of title sequences, combined with the specific textual requirements of credit presentation, liberated their designers to experiment with techniques that had not been widely adopted in mainstream American filmmaking at large. We can therefore see some of the title sequences described above as representing an advance guard of cinematic method that goes beyond their progressive and dynamic utilisation of widescreen formats. Indeed, they represent early and prominent examples of aesthetics that would come to be more widely adopted and eventually absorbed into the everyday language of New Hollywood cinema and beyond. While the emergence of widescreen was certainly not the only stimulus to adaptation and innovation, it provides a fruitful illustration of this process in action.

NOTES

1.   This essay is designed in part as a corrective to some errors made in my doctoral thesis: *Promises in the Dark: Opening Title Sequences in American Feature Films of the Sound Period* (University of East Anglia, 2001). Whereas my thesis drew largely on television and VHS viewing copies, the advent of DVD and broadband internet has brought enhanced opportunities to revisit widescreen films in their original ratios. Although a legal obligation not to crop credits means that widescreen title sequences have often been letter-boxed for presentation in a 4:3 format even when the rest of the film is panned and scanned, this has not invariably been the case.

2.   Joel W. Finler, *The Hollywood Story* (New York: Crown Publishers, 1988), 289.

3.   Finler, *The Hollywood Story*, 288.

4.   John Belton, *Widescreen Cinema* (Cambridge, Mass: Harvard University Press, 1992), 105.

5.   John Belton, "CinemaScope: The Economics of Technology", *Velvet Light Trap*, no. 21, summer 1985, 42; Keith M. Johnston, *Coming Soon: Film Trailers and the Selling of Hollywood Technology* (Jefferson, N.C.: McFarland, 2009), 27.

6.   Belton, *Widescreen Cinema*, 191.

7.   James Spellerberg, "CinemaScope and Ideology", *Velvet Light Trap*, no. 21, summer 1985, 31.

8.   Detractors included Howard Hawks, who felt CinemaScope was "good only for showing great masses of

movement" and Billy Wilder, who famously quipped that it was "a great process for filming the life of a dachshund". Charles Barr, "CinemaScope and After", in Gerald Mast and Marshall Cohen (eds.), *Film Theory and Criticism* (New York: Oxford University Press, 1974), 138–39; Wolfgang Kemp, "The Narrativity of the Frame", in Paul Duro (ed.), *The Rhetoric of the Frame* (Cambridge: Cambridge University Press, 1996), 13.

9. One far earlier 2D film that thrust its main title forward in exaggerated perspective was *The 39 Steps* (Alfred Hitchcock, 1935). However, it is worth noting that in this example the trajectory is over the viewer's right shoulder, which produces a very different effect from titles projected directly toward the viewer's face.

10. Richard Hincha, "Selling CinemaScope: 1953–1956", *Velvet Light Trap*, no. 21, summer 1985, 46.

11. Derek Elley, "Epic Entertainment", *The Movie*, vol. 4, chapter 41, 806.

12. It is worth noting that split-screen effects in title sequences pre-date the 1960s. Indeed, they were at the height of their popularity in the 1930s, when they were often used (particularly by Warner Bros.) to present two simultaneous vignettes of supporting characters during the corresponding actor credits.

13. In this essay I cite three films directed by Stanley Donen in which split-screen or other formal segmentation of the frame is used during the opening titles. It is worth noting that Donen also used split-screen effects in the main body of several films, including *It's Always Fair Weather* (1955, CinemaScope), *Funny Face* (1957, VistaVision), *Indiscreet* (1958, 1.85:1 ratio), *Damn Yankees* (1958, 1.85:1 ratio), *The Grass is Greener*, and *Charade* (1963, 1.85:1 ratio).

14. Sergio Dias Branco, "The Mosaic-Screen: Exploration and Definition", *Refractory*, vol. 14, December 2008, http://refractory.unimelb.edu.au/2008/12/27/the-mosaic-screen-exploration-and-definition-%E2%80%93-sergio-dias-branco.

15. Dias Branco, "The Mosaic-Screen".

16. See, for instance, André Bazin, "The End of Montage" and "A Little Late", *Velvet Light Trap*, no. 21, summer 1985, 14–16.
17. David Bordwell, "Widescreen Aesthetics and Mise en Scene Criticism", *Velvet Light Trap*, no. 21, summer 1985, 25.

First published in *Film International*, issue 74, vol. 13, no. 4 (2015), 6–19. DOI: 10.1386/fiin.13.4.6_1.

WOULD YOU CREDIT IT? THE OPENING TITLES OF AFTER THE FOX

When it comes to putting audiences in the right frame of mind to enjoy the film ahead, there are few tools as effective as a suitably themed opening title sequence. Hot on the heels of the wacky three-minute heist scene that launches *After the Fox* (Vittorio de Sica, 1966) comes a lively animated sequence set to a catchy theme song. It certainly does its bit to lift the spirits while whetting the appetite for another 100 minutes of anarchic tomfoolery.

For films of a comedic tone, cartoons set to a jaunty tune had long been a popular choice for enlivening the opening credits and animated titles can be found as far back as the silent period. There was no shortage of cartoons in title sequences of the thirties and forties; very few were animated, but the ones that were included some corkers. Look out for the playful and dapper serpent of *The Lady Eve* (Preston Sturges, 1942), for instance, or the terrified heroes shivering their bones to bits in *Abbott and Costello Meet Frankenstein* (Charles T. Barton, 1948).

It was not until the 1950s that animated titles took the industry by storm, however. When the American designer Saul Bass created a striking abstract animation for *The Man with the Golden Arm* (Otto Preminger, 1955), it met with widespread acclaim. After a string of other innovative and eye-catching title sequences, his witty six-minute animated epilogue for *Around the World in 80 Days* (Michael Anderson, 1956) helped to push the demand for inventive title sequences through the roof.

At around the same time, film music was changing too. The enormous success of the theme song to *High Noon* (Fred Zinnemann, 1952), coupled with a growing awareness of the business benefits of cross-promoting films and records, triggered a substantial rise in movie theme songs during the 1950s and 1960s, many of which played out over the opening credits. It was boom time for animated titles and theme songs alike. *After the Fox*, sporting title graphics designed by Maurice Binder and animated by Dick Horn to the accompaniment of a recently released Burt Bacharach and Hal David number peppily delivered by The Hollies, was right on trend.

Designer Maurice Binder, who had been born in New York in 1918, started creating film titles in the late 1950s—initially for American pictures, before taking a

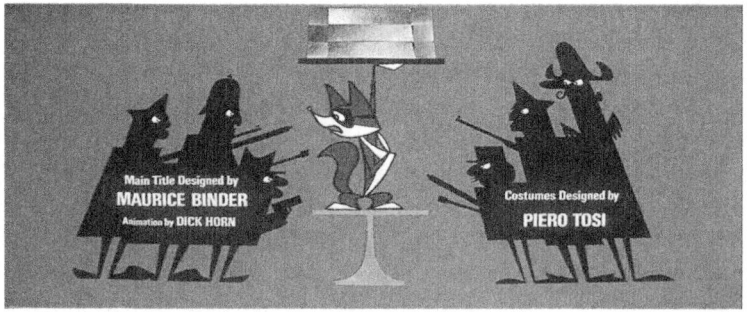

After the Fox (1966)

growing number of British commissions through the course of the 1960s. He first made his mark with the animated titles for *The James Dean Story* (George W. George and Robert Altman, 1957) but it was his iconic opening for *Dr. No* (Terence Young, 1962), which he followed with more than a dozen further openers for the James Bond franchise, that secured his reputation as one of the most celebrated title designers of all time.

The London-born Horn had started his career with the UK-based Halas and Batchelor company in 1946 before working his way round a string of other leading animation studios. Twenty years later, just about the time he was animating *After the Fox*, he was also working on segments of *The Beatles* television series. His later projects included animations for *Yellow Submarine* (George Dunning, 1968) and directing episodes of such affectionately remembered series as *The Charlie Brown and Snoopy Show*.

By the time *After the Fox* appeared, entertainingly animated titles had become practically *de rigeur* for Peter Sellers comedies. Its animal antics were prefigured in Maurice Binder's earlier sequence for *The Mouse that Roared* (Jack Arnold, 1959), where an adorable crown-wearing rodent symbolised the small European Duchy of Grand Fenwick. Then, in the intervening years, some of best title designers of the age, including Richard Williams and Robert Ellis, provided sparkling animated openers for such films as *Trial and Error* (James Hill, 1962), *The Wrong Arm of the Law* (Cliff Owen, 1963), *What's New Pussycat?* (Clive Donner, 1965), and *The Wrong Box* (Bryan Forbes, 1966). Most beloved of all, of course, was David DePatie and Friz Freleng's title sequence for *The Pink Panther* (Blake Edwards, 1963), which introduced a character so popular it spawned its own spin-off franchise.

The panther may have followed the mouse, but the fox was indubitably on the trail of the Pink Phink. The playful style of *After the Fox*'s title animation, in which its vulpine hero impishly interacts with the credit lettering, is clearly beholden to *The Pink Panther*, even while the film's poster artwork preferred to remind audiences that it followed the pussycat. Meanwhile, white-eyed silhouettes of the pursuing police evoke the trio of crooks in the titles to the first panther sequel, *A Shot in the Dark* (Blake Edwards, 1964). Colourful geometric patterns of dots and lines interspersed or combined with the character animation are more typical of Binder's other recent sequences and recall the abstract pop art qualities that are more fully developed in his work for such films as *Dr. No*, *Charade* (Stanley Donen, 1963), and *Arabesque* (Stanley Donen, 1966).

Sitting atop the crest of a stylistic wave that would crash down not long afterwards, the opening title sequence for *After the Fox* went largely unremarked by contemporary critics. Nevertheless, it certainly kicks off the film in splendid style and has, in recent years, come to be fondly remembered as evocative of an era.

First published in *After the Fox* (Blu-ray booklet) (British Film Institute, 2020), 10–13.

CATCH ME IF YOU CAN, AUTO FOCUS, FAR FROM HEAVEN, AND THE ART OF RETRO TITLE SEQUENCES

> *A title sequence is more than just a list of credits. It can be a mini-movie which sets up the film that it's a part of. It can establish mood, period and style. A title sequence can take care of backstory. It can soothe the audience or get them agitated. Title sequences are an art form of their own.*

> —Big Film Design[1]

Over the past few months we have been treated to a wave of American films that have taken as their source material the film styles and genres of times gone by. Films such as *Catch Me if You Can* (Steven Spielberg, 2002), *Far from Heaven* (Todd Haynes, 2002), *Chicago* (Rob Marshall, 2002), *Undercover Brother* (Malcolm D. Lee, 2002), and *Auto Focus* (Paul Schrader, 2002) have shared the agenda of lavishly recreating period features whilst positioning themselves explicitly within earlier cinematic traditions. Several of these films, including *Catch Me if You Can, Auto Focus*, and *Far from Heaven*, have announced their intentions from the very beginning, signalling their relationship to their antecedents by using title sequences that combine highly evocative images and musical scores. It is these films I will discuss in this article.

Each of these movies is located at a very specific point in time and space. Each is also characterised by its generic revisionism. *Far from Heaven* recreates the closeted suburban affluence of Eisenhower's America in 1957. In doing so it pays homage to classical Hollywood melodrama and, in particular, the films of director Douglas Sirk, whose 1955 movie *All That Heaven Allows* forms its explicit basis. *Catch Me if You Can* showcases the jet-setting new prosperity of the mid-late 1960s, at the same time revisiting the caper movie so popular at that time. *Auto Focus* charts a course from the clean-cut home entertainment industry of 1964 Los Angeles to the deterioration of family values and the rise of home porn in late 1960s and 1970s America, its focus on actor Bob Crane (Greg Kinnear) resurrecting the tradition of the celebrity biopic. In each film, the set and costume designs painstakingly emulate the fashions and décor of their respective eras. Nevertheless, they all derive their verisimilitude less from a bid for historical authenticity than from the cinematic heritage on which they draw.

All three films use their opening title sequence to signal from the outset the sensibility that defines them. To do so is a pervasive technique, as the above quotation from Big Film Design indicates. It has been widely used for decades, and is not in itself peculiar to revisionist movies. Examples range from the animated title sequence of *Move Over Darling* (Michael Gordon, 1963), which sets a sprightly tone and summarises the entire narrative through the witty orchestration of three wedding rings, to the 'creepy' lettering, oozing in front of a misty backdrop in *Voodoo Woman* (Edward L. Cahn, 1956), or the scratchy hand-lettering of *Berlin Horse* (Malcolm Le Grice, 1970). There, as David James has argued of many other avant-garde films, "authorship is inscribed not in the narrative or the imagery so much as in the self-consciously domestic manufacture".[2]

CATCH ME IF YOU CAN

Catch Me if You Can has been compared to "the light, sophisticated Cary Grant comedies of the 1950s and 1960s".[3] The tale of teenage con artist Frank Abagnale Jr. (Leonardo DiCaprio), ever metamorphosing his identity in the course of his relentless pursuit by an FBI agent Carl Hanratty (Tom Hanks), it opens with a title sequence that combines the chase motif with an aura of playfulness and excitement. Designed by Olivier Kuntzel and Florence Deygas for Nexus Productions, the sequence is a brightly coloured animation of geometrically stylised figures chasing one another through geometrically stylised scenery.

The sequence moves through a series of locations, from airport, to road, then poolside bar, a hospital, a library, and a wedding party, the colour scheme changing with each new setting. Little yellow arrows point to the silhouetted figures representing Frank and Hanratty, so that their progress can be tracked as the Frank figure subtly shifts identity from aeroplane pilot to doctor, and so forth. The figure of Hanratty gets ever closer as the sequence unfolds, until they finally share a frame during the producer credit. A fade out leaves the end of the tale open, upholding the suspense of the main film. Other whimsical pleasures are interspersed throughout the sequence, such as the jokey conjunction of technical credits with iconic items. For instance, the real Frank W. Abagnale, author of the book from which the film derives, is credited during the library sequence, and musician John Williams' credit is placed next to the image of a grand piano.

Catch Me if You Can (2002)

These titles have been widely noted by reviewers, who have likened them to DePatie-Freleng's celebrated animations for the Pink Panther films as well as more general design trends of 1960s titling such as the work of Saul Bass.[4] Comparisons might also be drawn with the Disney family comedy, *Emil and the Detectives* (Peter Tewksbury, 1964), with its three angular 'Skrinks', faceless, black-hatted and suited in front of a navy background. The technique of annexing technical credits to appropriate images has been used in a horde of earlier films. Fittingly, this ruse was especially prevalent during the 1950s and 1960s, where it can be found in such movies as *Houseboat* (Melville Shavelson, 1958), *To Kill a Mockingbird* (Robert Mulligan, 1962), and *Do Not*

Disturb (Ralph Levy, 1965).

Sight & Sound magazine went so far as to describe the title sequence of *Catch Me if You Can* as one of the film's two most striking features.[5] Such acclaim in itself recalls that which greeted the credits for *The Pink Panther* (Blake Edwards, 1963). Whilst Bosley Crowther's *New York Times* review of that earlier film was not altogether complimentary, he added,

> There is one thing about this picture that is clever and joyous at least. That is a cartooned pink panther that runs through the main titles at the start, making mischief with the lettering, insistently getting in the way. He is so blithe and bumptious, so sweet and entirely loveable that he's awfully hard to follow. It's questionable whether the picture does.[6]

Indeed, such was the panther's success that he starred in his own long-running cartoon series on television, spawning an ever-popular merchandising franchise. There is certainly no accident in the fact that *Catch Me if You Can*'s title sequence, like the rest of the film, makes unmistakable its relation to its forebears. Co-designer Olivier Kuntzel comes from a family with a strong design background and is brother to the French film academic and videomaker Thierry Kuntzel, who authored a detailed and insightful analysis of the opening title sequence of *The Most Dangerous Game* (Ernest B. Schoedsack and Irving Pichel, 1932).[7]

The wide critical acclaim that has greeted the titles of *Catch Me if You Can* is founded on several factors. Firstly, their style combines a startling modernity with a retro cool that powerfully recalls the light comedies of the 1960s. Its resemblance to *The Pink Panther*'s titles, achieved through the combination of visual imagery and a Henry Mancini-like score, offers a well-known point of reference that invokes the sprightly crime films so characteristic of that era. Secondly, it sets the tone perfectly for the tale that follows: a tale where pleasures arise no more from the story itself than from the telling of it. "Like Frank himself, *Catch Me if You Can* is restless and playful, forever trying out new styles", argues Geoffrey McNab.[8] The title sequence is just the first of these. Thirdly, and by no means least importantly, to watch the title sequence is a pleasurable experience in its own right. It may indeed prepare the audience for the main narrative but at the same time it provides an almost entirely separate work that contributes, like trailers and advertisements, to the diversity of the programme.

AUTO FOCUS

Auto Focus is a very different kind of film from *Catch Me if You Can*. It charts the personal and career trajectory of *Hogan's Heroes* star Bob Crane from wholesome family entertainment icon and devoted husband to a compulsive philanderer whose autoerotic obsession with home porn spirals out of control and in doing so destroys his career, family life, and personal relationships. The film, especially in its early parts, faithfully emulates the aesthetics of the world of 1960s film and television family entertainment, only later deviating from this style in order to represent the decay of that milieu's associated values. The title sequence, designed by Ken Ferris, acts as a point of connection between these parts, light in style and mood, but using motifs that anticipate Crane's personal free fall. The causes and means of his degeneration are thus present as latent images from the very beginning.

The title sequence's visuals mark both the period in which the film was set and the ironic distance the film upholds between that era and its point of production. In doing so, they evince an almost clinical detachment from the subject of the film. "For all its dedication to showing Bob's excesses and misapprehensions", argues Cynthia Fuchs,

> the film opens with credits, under Angelo Bada-lamenti's slick-jazzy score, that posit a peculiar distance from its subject. Martini glasses, bikinis and cigarette holders, Hugh Hefner and Polaroid cameras: the images designate an era, a place, a sense of insularity, ease, and privilege. And so: L.A., mythic land of pretty surfaces and preening affects.[9]

By establishing this cultural context from the start, the film is able to pithily convey its take on the main characters. It is their "absolute inability to see themselves", argues Fuchs, that "most clearly indicts Bob and John [Willem Dafoe]. Not as perverts per se, but as products of a culture premised on consumption and illusion, endless need and promise".[10] Nothing could signal this meaning more effectively than the title sequence that launches the film.

Like *Catch Me if You Can*, this sequence also exhibits debts to titling styles of the era depicted. It simply screams early 1960s, using a carefully choreographed array of silhouetted designs that move fluidly across the screen, overlapping with one another so as to provide a formal pleasure of semi-abstract animation, redolent of the animated jigsaw pieces that open *The Misfits* (John Huston, 1961). In the choice of shapes used, it further recalls *Rock All Night* (Roger Corman, 1957), whilst the

Auto Focus (2002)

sectioning of the screen into areas of pastel colour echoes *Portrait in Black* (Michael Gordon, 1960). As in *Catch Me if You Can,* and many title sequences of the late 1950s and 1960s, the first decade of widescreen cinema, the frame is emphatically a two-dimensional space, to be geometrically divided up and sectioned off, a flat canvas that attempts no illusion of scenic depth.

None of the title sequences of that period used a montage of contemporary artefacts in such a schematic way as *Auto Focus,* however. The first film to do so was probably designer Don Record's arresting collage of pop art and psychedelia in *How Sweet It Is!* (Jerry Paris, 1968). The titling of *Auto Focus* certainly finds its stylistic inspiration in contemporary artefacts but the way they are used is a product of the post-modern era, bearing closer relation to such recent montages as those adorning the 1998 book, *Atomic Cocktails.* This beautifully produced recipe book illustrates in every detail its argument that "the cocktail came to represent the unique American talent for combining disparate components into a final suitable product for mass consumption".[11]

The sequence can itself be seen as a cocktail in which commingled elements convincingly delineate both the milieu of the film and the complex interchange of agents that help determine the path of Crane's life. Just as the masterful plot summary achieved in the opening titles for *Catch Me if You Can* are most fully appreciated after viewing the whole film, so the credits for *Auto Focus* have an added resonance on a second viewing when the implications of the montage elements are fully recognised.

FAR FROM HEAVEN

Designed by Bureau, who had previously worked with director Todd Haynes to design the titles for his earlier films, *Safe* (1995) and *Velvet Goldmine* (1998), the titles for *Far from Heaven* are at the opposite end of the aesthetic pole from those of *Catch Me if You Can* and *Auto Focus*. The reason for this derives from the different era of filmmaking from which it draws its inspiration. In the way that the sequence relates to the main film, it fulfils some very similar functions though. *Far from Heaven* is an emotionally overblown melodrama with striking debts to Douglas Sirk. As well as adopting the main structure of his film *All That Heaven Allows*, it emulates its mise-en-scène, mimicking its stylised mode of speech and movement, as well as the cinematography.

The title sequence refers to *All That Heaven Allows* as explicitly as does the rest of the film. Brief by modern standards, the sequence groups several credits onto the screen at once, in the ubiquitous style of 1940s and 1950s cinema. The elegant copperplate lettering signals both a historical period and a genteel and restrained style of address. Behind the titles we are introduced to the mise-en-scène of richly coloured autumn leaves that forms the film's dominant visual motif. *All That Heaven Allows* had also used a crane shot to combine images of affluent small-town suburbia with the carmine leaves fluttering at the top of a tree and this repetition possesses a heady resonance. The title sequence simultaneously confirms the film's frame of reference for the cinephilic viewers who will recognise its source material, whilst the rich colours and Elmer Bernstein's lavish orchestral score create a heightened emotional environment that signal to all the sensibility of this singular viewing experience.

CONCLUSION

Each of the films discussed here has drawn on earlier titling styles to signal both an era and a filmmaking sensibility. In so doing, they have forged a contract with the audience at the outset, instructing them of the parameters within which the film operates, alerting them to the tonalities of the film to come, and encouraging them to approach that experience in a frame of mind where they will be receptive to the pleasures it has to offer.

In each case, this continued a project that began before the viewer set foot in the auditorium, as the title sequences shared common features with a range of publicity materials. The classic lettering style of *Far from Heaven* was used across its print and internet publicity. The same is true of the brightly coloured period design of *Auto Focus*, its poster dominated by a bikini-clad girl silhouetted in blue. A variation on the title animations dominate the website of *Catch Me if You Can*, and its chase motif appears in subtly varying ways on a range of promotional posters and print advertisements. These posters use pictures of the stars, Hanks and DiCaprio, instead of anonymous silhouettes, although one simulates motion blur to such an extent that the figures are identifiable only by the names printed above them. The promotional campaign, like the title sequence, combines an impression of perpetual motion with endlessly metamorphosing identity. The title sequences for each of these films may indeed be distinctive, but they are intrinsically part of the whole package, linking the viewing experience with the expectations generated by the studio publicity.

These films are by no means the first to use retro titling styles in order to signal their relation to earlier works. Nor is it the first time that a wave of films using this technique have been released at a specific point in time. The most distinctive cycle undoubtedly occurred in the late 1960s and early 1970s when a significant number of title sequences examined and adapted their design heritage, persistently flaunting technique and often foregrounding the act of addressing the audience. The popularity of these devices bore testimony to an increasing self-awareness in the field, a tendency more extensively characteristic of American films of the era. Perhaps the best known of these sequences is Saul Bass's opening for *That's Entertainment, Part II* (Gene Kelly, 1976), but other striking examples can be found in such films as *They Shoot Horses, Don't They?* (Sydney Pollack, 1969), *What's Up, Doc?* (Peter Bogdanovich, 1972), and *The Sting* (George Roy Hill, 1973). Whether films such as *Catch Me if You Can* and *Auto Focus* herald a new cycle of revisionist credit sequences remains to be seen, but there is no doubt that they represent inspiring additions to the varied and exciting developments that have occurred in film titling of recent years.

I would like to express my thanks to Charlotte Bavasso and Juliette Stern at Nexus Productions for their assistance in preparing this article.

NOTES

1. Big Film Design, www.bigfilmdesign.com (accessed 24 March 2003; quoted content now discontinued).
2. David E. James, *Allegories of Cinema: American Film in the Sixties* (Princeton: Princeton University Press, 1989), 144.
3. Nick James, "Out of the Pastiche", *Sight & Sound*, vol. 13, no. 3, March 2003, 3.
4. Peter Bradshaw, "*Catch Me if You Can*", *Guardian* (London): *Review*, 31 January 2003, https://www.theguardian.com/culture/2003/jan/ 31/artsfeatures4; Philip French, "*Catch Me if You Can*", *Observer*, 2 February 2003, https:// www.theguardian.com/film/2003/feb/02/philipfrench; James, "Out of the Pastiche", 3; Mick LaSalle, "*Catch Me if You Can*", *San Francisco Chronicle*, 25 December 2002, https://sfgate.com/movies/article/Holiday-Movies-Sit-back-and-enjoy-his-flight-2743359.php; Geoffrey McNab, "*Catch Me if You Can*", *Sight & Sound*, vol. 13, no. 3, February 2003, 40.
5. James, "Out of the Pastiche", 3.
6. Bosley Crowther, "*The Pink Panther*", *New York Times*, 24 April 1964, 25.
7. Thierry Kuntzel, "The Film-Work, 2", *Camera Obscura*, no. 5, spring 1980, 6-69.
8. McNab, "*Catch Me*", 40.
9. Cynthia Fuchs, "*Auto Focus*", *Nitrate Online*, 22 November 2002, https://nitrateonline.com/2002/rautofocus.html.
10. Fuchs, "*Auto Focus*".
11. Karen Brooks, Gideon Bosker, and Reed Darmon, *Atomic Cocktails: Mixed Drinks for Modern Times* (San Francisco: Chronicle Books, 1998), 9.

First published in *Senses of Cinema*, issue 26, May–June 2003. http://sensesofcinema.com/2003/feature articles/retro_titles.

FILM TITLE SEQUENCES IN THE TWENTY-FIRST CENTURY

The first two decades of the twenty-first century have seen significant developments in film titling trends. The most notable, with the most far-reaching implications for design strategy and audience experience alike, has been a rapid shift towards placing all or most of the credits at the end of the film—rather than at or near the start, as was the dominant practice during the twentieth century. In theatrical features, it would seem that the opening title sequence as an apparatus for easing and regulating the viewer's transition into the diegetic world is fast becoming an endangered species. Fewer and fewer films employ an opening title sequence at all and, of those that do, the majority adheres to a new norm characterised by brevity and minimalism.

This change is particularly conspicuous when considered in relation to concurrent developments in the arena of television title sequences, where the 'new golden age' of broadcast content, led by such subscription-based media giants as HBO and Netflix, has been matched by what many commentators have hailed as a 'golden age' of title sequences.[1] As Lance Richardson observes, "HBO has long aspired to dissolve the boundaries between cinema and your living room" and, as part of this process, began

> to insinuate prestige through opening sequences that echo the classic work of title designers like Kyle Cooper (*Se7en*), Dan Perri (*Star Wars*), and Saul Bass (*Vertigo*). To raise the brand, in effect, HBO co-opted and normalized a hallmark of iconic films: artistic openers that challenge the viewer to think more deeply about the following story.[2]

One might be forgiven for remarking a bitter irony in the coincidence of such appropriation of cinematic quality markers by television producers and the diminishing big-screen presence of the very innovations they have sought to emulate. If this is indeed the golden age of television title sequences then, statistically speaking, it is much harder to argue a similar case for opening titles in feature films. Yet this is not to say that the technical standards of film title sequences have slipped, nor that interesting work is no longer being produced, as I shall illustrate. Moreover, brevity and minimalism are not intrinsically bad. The most pertinent line of enquiry, I think, has less to do with questions of quality than with the need to reassess the purpose of a film's first minutes and how the structure of its opening can best serve audience experience and industrial incentives. With this in mind, ten years on from the first publication of my historical survey, "Beyond Saul Bass" (reprinted earlier in this volume), the time seems ripe to expand and update the observations therein and provide a fuller account of film titling in the twenty-first century.[3]

Rather than considering the shifts in titling styles and norms that have taken place during the past two decades as a complete sea change, it is more appropriate to look on them as trends that emerged and mutated from key developments that occurred during the late twentieth century. These include the dilution and eventual erasure of contractual obligations to give on-screen credit to designated cast and crew during an opening title sequence; an increased investment in logos and brand identity; huge leaps forward in digital technologies, among which the launch and rapid uptake of Adobe After Effects in the mid-1990s proved especially transformational; and the proliferation of independent motion design companies that this desktop revolution precipitated. Working in conjunction with the more recent emergence of new modes of film consumption and engagement that the advent of broadband internet and Wi-Fi has enabled, these factors, which had already begun to reshape film title design in critical ways, remain powerful drivers in film titling's ongoing evolution.

REASSESSING THE ROLE OF OPENING TITLE SEQUENCES

In order to locate the reasons underlying the early twenty-first century's prevailing trend towards brevity and minimalism in opening title sequences, it is instructive to recall the reasons they came into being in the first place. In the early days of cinema they served to mark copyright ownership and, with the emergence of the American studio system, soon assumed additional roles, including reinforcing the association of production companies, stars, writers, directors, and other crew with quality products. As longer narrative features became the most prestigious and marketable form of Hollywood entertainment, the title sequence's role in marking the start of the film (that is, signalling the moment at which the audience should get comfortable and pay attention) also became more important. As time went on, inflation of both the number of opening credits and their on-screen duration, as dictated by increasingly powerful trade unions, incentivised filmmakers to make more efficient use of the time during which the credits unfurled—guiding audience expectations by signalling elements such as genre and mood, and doing so in what were often very entertaining ways.

When considering contemporary developments, the importance of the relaxation in trade union agreements about how filmmakers must be credited cannot be over-stated. Now that placing credits at the start of the film is no longer obligatory and is a matter of filmmaker choice, two questions arise. The first is why filmmakers might elect to truncate the opening title sequence, or even omit it entirely. The second is whether the removal of credits entails the automatic sacrifice of the various additional roles title sequences have come to perform, or whether these duties can, in fact, be discharged perfectly well without them.

The primary motive for reducing opening credits appears relatively straightforward: they are contractually unnecessary and many viewers have expressed a distaste for them. Director Steven Spielberg has reported such negative attitudes as a finding of audience surveys.[4] Informally, we often see similar sentiments expressed in online chat forums, with many viewers keen to get to the 'meat' of the story, especially if they have already sat through a lengthy cinema pre-show ad reel. Changing modes of consumption on post-theatrical platforms have doubtless also had some effect, as credit titles can become difficult to read when streamed or downloaded onto mobile devices such as phones and tablets. Yet, if these factors seem like a compelling argument for consigning opening credits to the dustbin of history, what of the other functions the opening title sequence has so often served?

Perhaps the first thing to note is that the most long-standing form of on-screen credit—the production company logo or animated ident—has been the most resistant to erasure from the start of the spectatorial experience. Although copyright protections are enshrined elsewhere, it remains normal for production company idents, which usually exist as discrete and standardised audiovisual elements, to play before the unique film begins. That is, most are tacked onto the start of the film at hand instead of being incorporated within it—although the topical customisation of iconic studio idents occasionally provides a pleasurable variant on this practice. Indeed, whereas the twenty-first century has seen a drastic reduction in the number of opening credits to individual members of cast and crew, the opposite has been the case with production company credits. The growing complexity of film finance means it is now customary for a succession of production and distribution company idents to proceed the main film—a clipfest that can sometimes wear on for more than a minute. One additional function that this series of idents serves is the more traditional title sequence's longstanding role of marking the start of the feature presentation. This is a job it performs very adequately, irrespective of whether an integrated credits sequence and/or main title card follows.

If a unique opening title sequence is unnecessary as a basic marker of the start of a film, there still remains the question of what other changes may be wrought by its minimisation or absence. Let us first consider the credit titles themselves. The receipt of on-screen credit has long been important to cast and crew members for reasons such as career progression and entitlement to residual payments, but this applies whether the credits are placed at the start or the end of a film. Industrial considerations are therefore less pertinent, I think, than the ways the change may affect audience experience and expectation. Yet, here again, the reduction or omission of names in the opening title sequence is likely to have less impact than it might have done in earlier years.

In a rising proportion of cases, contemporary audiences will begin to watch a film, be it on the big screen or small, after a process of active selection. The proliferation of multiscreen cinemas and video on demand has widened viewers' choices, with a concomitant reduction in the likelihood that they will take a chance on a film of which they were previously unaware just because it happens to be scheduled at a convenient time. Most viewers will already know the name of the film, and whether it features their favourite performers or is, perhaps, the work of a favoured writer or director, before they start to watch it. In this sense, while opening credits may reinforce the pleasurable anticipation of witnessing a particular actor or director in action, they are unlikely to supply any particularly pressing new information.

When it comes to the other opening credits—those itemising the names of cast and crew members who are, at that moment in time, either unknown or of little interest to any given viewer—we might question how many will actually lodge in the viewer's mind in any case. Industry research has presumably been undertaken regarding typical audience memory of on-screen credits, although regrettably I have not located any such data in the public domain. My personal experience (which is, I imagine, far from unique) is that I register the names I already know and forget the rest immediately, so that if I want to find out who was responsible for a particularly strong performance or other achievement I need to look it up afterwards. End credits can, of course, satisfy this need more ably than opening credits, on top of which the internet era has made it very easy to find such information online. It would therefore seem that eradication of cast and crew names from a film's opening minutes is not, in itself, a devastating loss.

This brings us, at last, to the other fundamental role that opening title sequences have traditionally performed: that of generating an appropriate mood, and signalling apposite viewing templates, such as genre, that are intended to help audiences receive and experience films in the most positive ways possible. Few would argue against the continued importance of this aspect of a film's opening minutes. Interviewed in 2018, title designer Karin Fong explained, "We want people to take away a feeling. It's about a feeling and a tone, in the end", adding elsewhere (as paraphrased by the reporter), "a great title sequence should invite you in and the emotion it should evoke depends on what the story needs at that exact moment—from humor to suspense to an adrenaline rush".[5] But is this role really intrinsic to opening title sequences or can it be performed just as well in the absence of credit titles?

The functions Fong describes are commonly served by filmic elements other than the titles themselves, although strong associations attached to particular lettering styles (such as Playbill, often used in Western movies) have traditionally played a significant part in this process and, where present, still do so today. Thus, scaling down or dispensing with the credit lettering reduces the film-makers' palette but it does not preclude the possibility of effective viewer orientation; a large part of this job is frequently undertaken by other areas of the image, whether the material is narrative or non-narrative, and by music, speech, and sound, be it diegetic or non-diegetic. In the next part of this essay, I look at some examples of films that have been well served in this respect, despite beginning without any credit titles at all, or with a far more limited number than was typical through most of the twentieth century. Afterwards, I turn my attention to some films that have bucked the dominant trend and which feature more striking or elaborate opening title sequences than the majority of their contemporaries.

BREVITY AND MINIMALISM

I will begin with a recent example. Presentations of *Maze Runner: The Death Cure* (Wes Ball, 2018) open with the latest iteration of the iconic Twentieth Century Fox ident, after which the movie begins with a short series of establishing shots before swiftly launching the audience into an adrenaline-pumping action sequence. Almost eleven minutes pass after the end of the Fox ident before the appearance of the first and only opening title, "The Death Cure". In a fleeting reference to the film's back-story, its arrival coincides with the momentary flash of a solar flare, after which the words remain on screen for approximately eight seconds before seemingly receding into the dark depths of outer space. Title sequences don't get much briefer than this. Nevertheless, a great deal of information is conveyed during the film's opening min-

Maze Runner: The Death Cure (2018)

utes—embodied partly in the rhetoric of the extended pre-title sequence and partly in this pithy title card.

It seems fair to assume that a high proportion of the prospective audience for this picture would have considerable pre-awareness of the kinds of pleasure its makers aspired to offer and the viewing schema most conducive to their own enjoyment of the spectatorial experience. Adapted from one of a best-selling series of young adult science-fiction novels that first launched in 2009, *Maze Runner: The Death Cure* was the highly anticipated final instalment of a film trilogy that had already seen its first two entries top the American box office charts in 2014 and 2015. Such a lineage certainly goes a long way towards alleviating the burden of orienting the viewer in the opening minutes, whether in a title sequence or otherwise. Instead, the protracted and visceral pre-title sequence offers immediate gratification to audiences whose tastes have already been whetted by earlier franchise entries and pre-release promotional materials. Without any opening credits, the filmmakers succeed admirably in fulfilling the requirements Fong identifies for a great title sequence: "evoking the emotion the story needs at that exact moment". Eleven weeks after the film's global theatrical release, the effectiveness of this opening sequence was further ratified when Twentieth Century Fox issued it online as a promotional taster for the upcoming home entertainment release—a clip that has, at time of writing, garnered more than a million views on the studio's official YouTube channel.

Placed at the conclusion of the opening action sequence, the film's brief title card serves as a cinematic punctuation mark (or something, perhaps, more equivalent to a page break and chapter title), which helps to demarcate the transition to the next scene. In this respect, it is worth noting that contemporary shifts in the visual aesthetic and duration of opening title sequences have been attended by changes in music and sound design. Like many other movies featuring a pre-title sequence followed by a single title card, the main title is accentuated by an abstract sound effect of an approximately matching duration. The title card has further roles beyond partition, however. *Maze Runner: The Death Cure* provides ample illustration of a titling trend that had become a significant presence as far back as the 1980s: logotype as the lynchpin of brand identity.

The late twentieth century was, as Paul Grainge has observed in his discussion of evolving Hollywood production company logos, "a period in which branding had become an especially powerful imperative for both new and established media companies, serviced by a flourishing number of brand consultants, logo specialists and graphic design boutiques".[6] This trend affected movie marketing as much as it did corporate identity, especially for pictures belonging to existing or prospective franchises. Just as films such as *E.T. The Extra Terrestrial* (Steven Spielberg, 1982), *Ghostbusters* (Ivan Reitman, 1984), and *Back to the Future* (Robert Zemickis, 1985) employed highly distinctive title treatments that forged close links between the movies, their marketing materials, spin-off merchandise, and, in the latter cases, subsequent sequels, so the title treatment of *Maze Runner: The Death Cure* references earlier franchise entries. Indeed, such was the strength of the existing brand that the filmmakers did not deem it necessary to include the film's full name on the title card, which features only the name of the individual episode.

In the twenty-first century, the use of the title treatment to create and reinforce brand identity has become increasingly important; it is now common for the title treatments of eagerly anticipated movies to receive high-profile media launches.[7] As well as linking the film with publicity materials and ancillary products, in the era of ubiquitous social media main titles contribute, as Valentina Re points out, "to creating 'networked communities' or 'brand communities' based on a shared passion for media content".[8] A distinctive title treatment is not solely the province of blockbusters and franchise entries, however; it plays a key role in numerous marketing campaigns for films made in a range of genres and across the budgetary spectrum. Nor is it entirely confined to films in which opening credits have been dispensed with; recent examples can also be found in the longer and relatively traditionalist opening title sequences for such contrasting pictures as *The Beguiled* (Sofia Coppola, 2017) and *Sorry to Bother You* (Boots Riley, 2018). In each of these examples, the title treatment connects with marketing assets while also serving as an indicator of the film's genre and tone.[9]

Maze Runner: The Death Cure, like many other contemporary films, wraps up with what has come to be known as a 'main-on-end' sequence. After the narrative concludes, the key credits are displayed prominently, using the same typographic style as the title treatment, before a small-print crawl through the remaining technical credits marks the moment at which most viewers will generally choose to depart the auditorium or press the 'stop' button. This particular example provides very little encouragement for audiences to keep watching after the story ends. In a significant number of other cases, by contrast, the migration of credit titles from the film's beginning to its end has been accompanied by substantial investment in keeping viewers entertained—both as an incentive to stay and read the credits and as a pleasurable moment of emergence from the spectatorial experience. "The movie doesn't end on the final frame", argues designer Erin Sarofsky. "It ends really after the director is kind of finished having his way with you, so to speak. So it's like the sorbet at the end of the meal. Can't skip the sorbet!"[10]

Throughout this anthology, my focus has been on opening title sequences, and the ways in which they are designed to prepare audiences for the viewing experience ahead, but the growing prevalence of the 'main-on-end' merits a few further words in relation to their implications for the style and structure of opening titles. The key effect of upending the presentation of credits has been to package the film experience differently. The most high-profile, and arguably most successful, adoption of this practice can be found in films of the 'Marvel Cinematic Universe' (MCU), a franchise launched by Marvel Studios in 2008. Before considering this particular group of films, it is worth taking a brief step back to some of the earlier adaptations of Marvel properties produced during the course of the previous decade.

Among the earlier titles were a successful X-Men trilogy (2000-2006) and Spider-Man trilogy (2002-2007), within which each film opened with a sequence of striking digital animation. The X-Men openers, despite including only production company credits and main titles, each last around 45 to 60 seconds and all feature an exhilarating and enthralling forward rush through inner space, with the sequels offering variants on Robert Dawson's dazzling design for the first series entry. The Spider-Man films, by contrast, include a full complement of opening credits. All three sequences were designed by Kyle Cooper, with the sequels referencing the three-dimensional animated web motif he created for the first movie, after which they introduce new visual elements that hark back to narrative incidents from that first film and, in the process, call to mind the panels of the comic books from which the series derives. In each trilogy, the opening title

sequences convey a clear message. Their graphic and musical styles serve to bind the films together into discrete
sets and to assure viewers that the relationship of the
sequels to preceding films will entail both semblance and
difference; as with film genres, new entries promise exactly
the same pleasures as their predecessors while also re-
freshing them with additional delights.

With the release of *Iron Man* (Jon Favreau, 2008),
Marvel Studios took a further step. Here, discreet production company logos play over a diegetic establishing
shot. The movie then proceeds into the first action scene
without even a main title; all credits appear during an
animated main-on-end sequence. More significantly, the
end credits are followed by a short 'easter egg'—in this
case, a 22-second scene featuring a surprise appearance
from Nick Fury (Samuel L. Jackson). Fury informs Tony
Stark/Iron Man (Robert Downey Jr.) that he has come to
talk to him about "the Avenger Initiative". In a revelation
calculated to whet the appetite of film fans for upcoming
franchise instalments, he explains, "You've just become
part of a bigger universe. You just don't know it yet."
With these words, the 'Marvel Cinematic Universe' was
launched. Subsequent MCU films have followed a similar
structure; in each case, the narrative is sandwiched
between a subtly evolving Marvel Studios animated ident
and a main-on-end credits sequence topped off by an
easter egg—with the latter element invariably exciting
much discussion and speculation among fan communities.

The MCU films, in contrast to earlier Marvel adaptations such as the original X-Men and Spider-Man trilogies,
locate the credits within a structure designed to direct
the viewer's anticipation towards future franchise entries
rather than helping to orient them towards the imminent
experience of the particular film they are about to watch.
The consequent impression is that these films, which

also feature intersecting characters and story elements, should not be thought of as self-contained narratives, nor consumed in such a way, but rather as jigsaw pieces within the grander MCU scheme—a rhetoric calculated to increase appetite for, and consumption of, further franchise products.

Through the course of the early twenty-first century, sequels and franchise entries have steadily increased their grip on box office share, yet they still represent just a small proportion of film releases. Thus, recent years have also seen other pictures that, like *Maze Runner: The Death Cure*, retain a brief opening title sequence (sometimes featuring just a single card) but do so in ways designed to serve the film's individual qualities instead of reinforcing franchise credentials. One very elegant example is Picture Mill's design for *Phantom Thread* (Paul Thomas Anderson, 2017), in which the sinuous twists and knots and overwrought intricacy of the main title card foreshadow the film's general style and tone as well as the behaviour and relationships of its lead characters. Another example, which hails from the same design studio,

Phantom Thread (2017)

is *Hitchcock* (Sacha Gervasi, 2012), where a pre-title sequence in which the eponymous director (Anthony Hopkins) stands in front of the iconic Bates' mansion from *Psycho* (Alfred Hitchcock, 1960) is followed by a main title card that apes the distinctive letterforms of *Psycho*'s original poster artwork. Whereas each of these examples features eye-catching lettering, *Three Billboards Outside Ebbing, Missouri* (Martin McDonagh, 2017) demonstrates that quiet understatement can be equally effective in helping to set the tone. Here, a spartan white-on-back main title card quietly separates a succession of shabby, broken-down billboards standing bleakly in the mist from the sunlit narrative sequence that ensues.

As these cases show, the twenty-first century tendency towards brevity and minimalism in opening title sequences does not strip the films' first moments bare of all their signalling properties. Even where films have no main title or opening credits at all, the decision to begin the movie in such a way can, in it its own right, tacitly suggest a suitable framework for consumption. There are many ways to open a film well and, as contemporary filmmakers have amply demonstrated, an extended title sequence is only one of them.

PERSISTENCE OF VISION

Not all twenty-first century films have followed the overarching movement away from striking and elaborate opening title sequences. Although those employing full-length opening credits are now in a minority, and the wave of complex digital animations that enlivened so many openings in the late 1990s and early 2000s, especially within the sci-fi genre, has subsided into intermittent ripples, there remains a considerable body of opening title sequences featuring a dazzling array of thought-provoking ideas and inventive styles and techniques.

A substantial number of these are informed in some way by the titling traditions of earlier eras. There are also others, of course, which are inspired simply by a more general logic of opening the film in whatever way seems most conducive to a positive viewer experience. Nevertheless, the high proportion of contemporary full-length sequences that follow long-established practices or respond to earlier traditions merits a closer look. It is noticeable that these often fall into at least one of two groups, which I will discuss in turn.

The first group is comprised of retro title sequences—some examples of which I have already examined in an earlier essay.[11] The second is associated with the films of auteur directors who, for the most part, first secured their reputations during the last thirty years of the twentieth century. From the film school-educated 'movie brat' generation to the indie boom of the 1990s, these filmmakers positioned themselves as fresh and distinctive voices, even as they flaunted their deep knowledge of, and affection for, earlier films and filmmaking traditions.

Although retro title sequences are not unique to the twenty-first century (the first cycle of parody and pastiche accompanied the generic revisionism of the late 1960s and 1970s) their second surge of popularity stands out all the more clearly in the context of the overall decline in full-length opening title sequences. Among contemporary title sequences taking this approach, the styles and reference points are richly diverse, as are the specific motivations for following this route. In some cases, filmmakers use such intertextual referencing merely to signal a period setting, but in many of the more interesting and rewarding examples it is designed to evoke a particular mood or sensibility, irrespective of the era in which the story takes place.

A disproportionate number of retro title sequences feature some form of animation, be it representational or abstract. One of my personal favourites is Geefwee Boedoe's design for *Monsters, Inc.* (Pete Docter, 2001): a witty and playful 2D animation in a markedly different style from the state-of-the-art technique of the main part of the film. Bright abstract shapes on a black background transform into the various components of a door (panels, knob, and so forth). This door opens twice in quick succession: first to show an ordinary closet, and then again to reveal the gullet of a roaring monster. It then zips off the screen to be replaced by a succession of brightly coloured doors that dance to a lively jazz score before lining themselves in rows and opening to reveal the letters of the first credit title. A weird and spindly monster arm reaches from another doorway to add a word in chalk, before an even bigger monster arm stretches out from a door on the opposite side of the screen and pulls away the credits to the apparent consternation of his predecessor, who promptly drops his chalk and disappears. As other titles tumble out of doors to be eaten or rearranged by a series of monsters, Friz Freleng's seminal animation for *The Pink Panther* (Blake Edwards, 1963) is called to mind. Yet this is no mere pastiche. Instead, it cleverly sets the tone for the film while anticipating its main conceit, which is that the monsters that hide in the closet are far less scary that reputed, and can, in fact, be rather funny and loveable. On top of this, it gestures towards one of the features that underlies Pixar films' immense popularity with audiences of all ages: the studio's exemplary fusion of child-pleasing material with a broad range of cultural references for the delectation of adult viewers.

Kiss Kiss Bang Bang (Shane Black, 2005) is an acclaimed example of a retro title sequence that employs animation to non-comic effect. Danny Yount's striking

Kiss Kiss Bang Bang (2005)

design dextrously blends mid-century influences with more contemporary graphic styles that suit the hybrid nature of a movie "based in part" on a 1941 crime novel. Incorporating images that occasionally hint at influences ranging from Maurice Binder's Bond title sequences to Saul Bass's poster for *Vertigo* (Alfred Hitchcock, 1958), it also encompasses such classic markers of pulp crime as lipstick marks, blood spatters, and bullet holes—all bound together by a colour palette dominated by black, muted red, grey, and cream, and a distinctively 1960s-styled score.

A decade later, Black opened his third theatrical feature, *The Nice Guys* (2016), with another retro animation. This sequence, designed by Gary Mau, signals the film's 1977 setting by means of a vivid orange colour scheme, period-style typography, and dominantly abstract animations that tie in ingeniously with the lettering style—all of which is accompanied by a funky seventies score. *Superbad* (Greg Mottola, 2007), by contrast, is a contemporary high school comedy that uses 1970s referents purely to set a tone that blends nostalgia with the 'retro cool' so beloved of self-styled outsiders. Opening with degraded footage of Columbia Pictures' long-obsolete 1976-1980 logo, this title sequence proceeds through a series of colourful silhouettes of the main characters dancing to the accompaniment of the first of several vintage soundtrack entries—The Bar-Kays' 1976 R&B album track, 'Too Hot to Stop'.

Of course, there are many ways besides animation in which retro title sequences can signal a period setting or sensibility. A simple but effective example can be found in *The Killer Inside Me* (Michael Winterbottom, 2010). For this neo noir, adapted from Jim Thompson's 1952 Texas-set pulp novel, the British design boutique Central Station created a stylish opening in which they overlaid monochrome photographs of the characters and locations with colourful filters in serpentine, abstract shapes. Their goal was to "help transport the viewer into the time period, colour palette, atmosphere and mood of the film [... using] our own contemporary take on classic '50's title sequences, that would set up the idealistic, yet hint at the undercurrent of the sinister".[12] In this sequence, Playbill lettering picks up the old-time associations of the small-town Western setting while the accompanying song, Little Willie John's 1956 hit recording of 'Fever', plays a powerful role in conveying the film's emotional timbre as well as foreshadowing the story's end.

Live-action retro title sequences can also serve as a

The Killer Inside Me (2010)

potent proclamation of a film's period setting or of its reference and response to earlier cinematic traditions. We can find an example in Ivar Edding's opening titles for the lurid 1989-set Cold War espionage thriller *Atomic Blonde* (David Leitch, 2017), which makes effective use of garish '80s-styled and coloured credit titles while, here again, a song from that decade provides further orientation. *Django Unchained* (Quentin Tarantino, 2012) goes further still; the title song and lettering style are direct quotations from *Django* (Sergio Corbucci, 1966), subtly refreshed through the use of a contemporary font for the second word of the main title.

As Alexandre Tylski et al. demonstrate in the French-language anthology, *Les Cinéastes et leurs génériques*, innovative and engaging title sequences, including their structures and the ways they relate to the film ahead, are often as closely associated with film directors as they are with title designers.[13] The final set of title sequences I will discuss is the noticeable cluster of idiosyncratic, full-length openers associated with auteur directors—an even more diverse group than the retro sequences described above, with which they sometimes overlap.

Several of the most acclaimed American directors to make their names in the 1970s and 1980s, such as Martin Scorsese, Spike Lee, Tim Burton, and the Coen Brothers, forged long-term creative relationships with some of the foremost title designers of the late twentieth century. Although many of these sequences bear the distinguishing trademarks of their designers, the longstanding commitment these directors have made to using title sequences in interesting and challenging ways has helped to imprint their films with their own personal marks of style and authorship.

Some members of this generation have subsequently followed the trend towards more minimalist opening credits. Scorsese, barring an eerily atmospheric minute-long title sequence for *Shutter Island* (2010), virtually abandoned opening credits after Saul and Elaine Bass's tour-de-force contribution to *Casino* (1995), while Lee's last feature to include a full-length opening title sequence was *Da Sweet Blood of Jesus* (2014). Yet there are also others that continue to prosper from title sequences that are as eye-catching as they are tonally and thematically apt. Even as their burgeoning box office success, and the resultant growth in the production budgets at their command, has seen much of their work absorbed into the commercial mainstream, the preponderance of attention-grabbing title sequences among their more recent releases remains a strident declaration of their bold individualism.

Within this group, several directors, including Tim Burton and the Coen Brothers, have continued to pursue creative relationships with particular designers. Across a period of almost twenty years, the majority of Burton's opening title sequences were designed by Robert Dawson until his retirement after *Alice in Wonderland* (2010). Since 2007, Burton has paired three times with industry veteran Richard Morrison, with whom he first worked on *Batman* (1989) more than thirty years ago, and twice with Matt Curtis. From the grand guignol of Morrison's title design for *Sweeney Todd* (2007) to Curtis's creepy concoction for *Miss Peregrine's Home for Peculiar Children* (2016), these sequences have followed such classic Dawson creations as *Edward Scissorhands* (1990), *Ed Wood* (1994), and *Sleepy Hollow* (1999) as they continue to announce and cement Burton's own particular brand of gothic. The Coens, for their part, have enjoyed a long and fruitful relationship with Randy Balsmeyer, who has created the title sequences for all of their features since *Miller's Crossing* (1990). From the vibrant animations of *O Brother, Where Art Thou?* (2000) and *Intolerable*

Cruelty (2003), through the apt austerity of *A Serious Man* (2009), and the gentle nostalgia of *Inside Llewyn Davis* (2013), these sequences have consistently provided pertinent and often amusing introductions to the stories at hand. Even in the Coens' most recent pictures, *Hail, Caesar!* (2016) and *The Ballad of Buster Scruggs* (2018), which partake of the general trend towards eschewing opening credits, the design of the main titles and the sequences in which they are positioned stand out in witty and entertaining ways.

Other seasoned auteurs, such as Sam Raimi and Paul Schrader, have no regular affiliation with any particular designer or design company but are equally dedicated to using opening title sequences in arresting and sometimes provocative ways. Raimi, who has presented us with memorable title sequences as far back as *The Evil Dead*

Oz The Great and Powerful (2013)

(1981), has continued to explore the possibilities of the form into the twenty-first century. After collaborating with Kyle Cooper on the aforementioned Spider-Man trilogy, he worked with Picture Mill, which provided the gloriously macabre opening title sequence for *Drag Me to Hell* (2009). Later, Garson Yu would design an equally beguiling title sequence for *Oz The Great and Powerful* (2013). This black-and-white, academy-ratio animation anticipates key elements of the story by combining motifs of Victorian paper theatres, nineteenth-century optical toys, the early cinematic illusionism of Georges Méliès, and the iconic tornado of *The Wizard of Oz* (Victor Fleming, 1939).

Schrader, meanwhile, has remained firmly committed to his belief that "one of the things an audience wants in the opening moments of a film is the sense that someone is in control".[14] We can see this demonstrated in the retro animations that open *Auto Focus* (2002); the sinuous and mysterious long take in which the camera explores the fringes of a room in *The Walker* (2007)—a sequence strongly redolent of the opening titles to *The Comfort of Strangers* (1990); the series of still photographs of closed and crumbling movie theatres that draws us into *The Canyons* (2013); and the excruciatingly slow movement

The Canyons (2013)

through a leafless winter landscape towards the sombre and forbidding doors of the eponymous church in *First Reformed* (2017). In each case, the title sequence skilfully establishes an appropriate tone while also introducing an element of intrigue.

The penchant for ostentatious or unconventional title sequences observable in the oeuvres of such directors as these is followed through in the work of a slightly later generation that came to feature direction only in the 1990s—by which time contractual obligations to include full opening credits were already rapidly eroding, even as frictions with the Writers Guild escalated over the bur-geoning use of directorial possessory credits.[15] Many title sequences for the films of directors such as Wes Anderson, Nicolas Winding Refn, Quentin Tarantino, and Edgar Wright (all of whom made their feature debuts between 1992 and 1996) bespeak the directors' ambitions to appro-priate, revive, and update bygone filmmaking traditions for a new generation while, at the same time, aspiring to the status of the previous era's canonised auteurs. A few of the numerous and varied opening title sequences to win popular and critical acclaim in recent years are those of *Death Proof* (Quentin Tarantino, 2007), *Fantastic Mr. Fox* (Wes Anderson, 2009), *Scott Pilgrim vs. The World* (Edgar Wright, 2010), *Drive* (Nicolas Winding Refn, 2011), *Moonrise Kingdom* (Wes Anderson, 2012), *The Grand Budapest Hotel* (Wes Anderson, 2014), *The Neon Demon* (Nicolas Winding Refn, 2016), and *Baby Driver* (Edgar Wright, 2017). Among the more recent industry entrants to keep the same torch burning is director Jason Reitman, whose eight collaborations with the husband-and-wife design team Gareth Smith and Jenny Lee have furnished the arresting opening titles for *Thank You for Smoking* (2005), *Juno* (2007), *Young Adult* (2011), *The Front Runner* (2018), and more.

Juno (2007)

THE FINAL WORDS?

The first two decades of the twenty-first century have, as we have seen, been principally characterised by the migration of credits from the start to the end of the film. Not only do many filmmakers now eschew the inclusion of cast and crew names at the outset, but fewer and fewer pause even to name the movie on screen. Is this a good thing or a bad thing?

The traditional point of view is that opening title sequences should be designed to serve the needs of the film at hand. From that perspective, we must surely admit that a good opening is a good opening, whether or not it includes any titles. Brief and minimalist title sequences, such as that of *Phantom Thread*, can help set a tone just as effectively as can the longer ones replete with main credits. If title sequence aficionados feel a sense of loss at the dwindling number of films featuring full opening credits, such regrets are not because contemporary filmmakers have lost their ability to connect with their audiences from the outset; it is because of the gradual stripping of stylistic diversity from the fringes of Hollywood cinema at large. Over the years, many people have come to celebrate the bold heterogeneity of titling styles that, even in some of their simplest forms, both oppose and enrich the conventional spectrum of narrational modes. Looked at in this way, opening title sequences collectively amount to a repository of non-normative techniques that are more closely aligned with such audiovisual forms as music videos and advertising than they are with mainstream narrative cinema. A widespread appetite for consuming title sequences outside of their intended contexts is plainly evident from the proliferation of online collections and video playlists.

With regard to how well different kinds of title sequences work in situ, Martin Scorsese hit the crux of the issue in a 1990 interview. "I like credits", he declared. "They promise something—like posters [...]. For me credit sequences are sometimes more important than the movie [...] because they present the picture a certain way." But he then went on to add, "I tend to get impatient with the title sequences that are unimaginative—that are just shown over shots of people driving, going in their house. I think in that case, don't do that. In that case, put white on black, put some music over it, and it's even nicer. It's much more honest about it. Then get the story started because you're wasting story time."[16]

The early twenty-first century has seen an accelerated polarisation between films in which the opening titles are brief and minimalist, or even non-existent, and those where filmmakers continue to celebrate and exploit the opportunities offered by longer and stylistically innovative title sequences. The main loss, measured according to quantity rather than any commonly held notions of quality, has been precisely the kinds of unimaginative title sequences Scorsese criticised—a turn of events expedited by industry agreements to make opening credits optional instead of mandatory. Nowadays, we can enjoy the best of both worlds, with filmmakers free to beguile us with a fabulous title sequence or else launch us straight into the story as they see fit. Whatever balance between these two approaches future years may bring, such artistic flexibility can only be a good thing.

NOTES

1. See, for instance, Jennifer Ouellette, "Credit Where Credit is Due", *Ars Technica*, 30 December 2019. https://arstechnica.com/gaming/2019/12/the-2010s-were-a-veritable-golden-age-of-opening-credits-in-television/; John Sellers, "TV's Golden Age of Opening Credits", *Salon*, 18 February 2012. https://www.salon.com/2012/02/18/tvs_golden_age_of_opening_credits/; Jason Tanz, "How TV Opening Titles Got to Be So Damn Good", *Wired*, 23 March 2017. https://www.wired.com/2017/03/tv-opening-titles-got-damn-good/.
2. Lance Richardson, "Opening Act", *The Verge*, 5 July 2017. https://www.theverge.com/2017/7/5/15886698/tv-title-sequence-history-sopranos-american-gods-netflix-skip.
3. Deborah Allison, "Beyond Saul Bass: A Century of American Film Title Sequences", *Film International*, 30 January 2011, http://filmint.nu/?p=202.
4. N.B., "Title Sequences in Film: A Deficit of Credits", *The Economist*, 25 January 2013. https://www.economist.com/prospero/2013/01/25/a-deficit-of-credits.
5. Ana Gómez Bernaus, "Type and Title Sequences: An Interview with Karin Fong", *Creative Cloud*, 11 May 2018. https://creativecloud.adobe.com/discover/article/type-and-title-sequences-an-interview-with-karin-fong; Hilda Saffari, "The Most Iconic Movie Title Sequences of All Time. And Why They Work", *frame.io*, 4 June 2018. https://blog.frame.io/2018/06/04/iconic-movie-title-sequences/.
6. Paul Grainge, "Branding Hollywood: Studio Logos and the Aesthetics of Memory and Hype", *Screen*, vol. 45, no. 4, winter 2004, 344.
7. See, for instance, Marvel Studios (@MarvelStudios),

Twitter post, 21 July 2019. https://twitter.com/MarvelStudios/status/1152751492555669504.

8. Valentina Re, "From Saul Bass to Participatory Culture: Opening Title Sequences in Contemporary Television Series", *NECSUS*, spring 2016. https://necsus-ejms.org/saul-bass-participatory-culture-opening-title-sequences-contemporary-tv-series/.

9. For further discussion of these examples see Eliza Brooke, "How to Capture the Feeling of a Movie in a Single Font", *Vox*, 12 November 2018. https://www.vox.com/the-goods/2018/11/12/18071808/suspiria-sorry-to-bother-you-the-favourite-title-design; Chris Thilk, "Movie Marketing Madness: *The Beguiled*", *Chris Thilk* (blog), 22 June 2017. https://christhilk.com/2017/06/22/the-beguiled-marketing/.

10. CBS News, "Giving Credit: The Creators of Movie Title Sequences", *CBS News*, 26 February 2017. https://www.cbsnews.com/news/giving-credit-the-creators-of-movie-title-sequences/.

11. Deborah Allison, "*Catch Me if You Can, Auto Focus, Far from Heaven*, and the Art of Retro Title Sequences", *Senses of Cinema*, issue 26, May–June 2003. http://sensesofcinema.com/2003/feature-articles/retro_titles.

12. Central Station Art, "*The Killer Inside Me* Titles", *Vimeo*, 8 May 2013. https://vimeo.com/65785680.

13. Alexandre Tylski (ed.), *Les Cinéastes et leurs génériques* (Paris: Editions L'Harmattan, 2008).

14. Kevin Jackson (ed.), *Schrader on Schrader & Other Writings* (London: Faber and Faber, 1990), 147.

15. Directors Guild of America, "Possessory Credit Timeline", *DGA Quarterly*, February 2004. https://www.dga.org/Craft/DGAQ/All-Articles/0402-Feb-2004/Possessory-Credit-Timeline.aspx.

16. T.J. English, "Martin Scorsese on Framing", *Blank on Blank*, 12 August 2016. https://allarts.org/programs/blank-on-blank/blank-blank-scorsese/.

First published in this anthology.

BOOK REVIEW:
UNCREDITED: GRAPHIC DESIGN AND OPENING TITLES IN MOVIES

By Gemma Solana and Antonio Boneu
Barcelona: Index Book, 2007

A more apt title could hardly be found for a book that
helps to expose the great injustice that saw the creators of
many thousands of highly accomplished film title sequences disappear into unacknowledged obscurity. Gemma
Solana and Antonio Boneu's *Uncredited* examines the
crucial role that these graphic artists played in shaping
our appreciation of the movies. In addition to its helpfully
annotated images, it also contains a substantial written
account that addresses many of the titling styles that
have been used since the inception of cinema. Boasting
over three hundred large format, full-colour glossy pages
containing many hundreds of high-quality film stills,
Uncredited is, in many respects, a dream come true for
both casual and serious enthusiasts of film title design.

Solana, head of Artimaña graphic design studio, and
Boneu, a cinema historian and television script writer/
director, must be commended for compiling a consider-

able quantity of information about the history of film title design and those who have contributed to its rich diversity. Their account of title design prior to the mid-1950s, when the now-legendary Saul Bass entered the field, is especially valuable, since these sequences have been relatively neglected in favour of his work and the other overtly authored pieces that have followed. Their success in identifying the uncredited designers of these earlier titles constitutes a genuine contribution to the evolving scholarship in the field.

Given these considerable strengths, it is disappointing that the book is not better written. The overall structure of the book works well, comprising ten chapters that focus variously on genres of titling style and the work of three generations of title designers. Individual chapters are often far less logically organised, however, bouncing between topics with a breathtaking abandon that sometimes makes them quite frustrating to read. The text is marred further by poor translation from a Spanish original; the finer points of the argument are sometimes hard to follow. Often, names of people—and, less frequently, of films—are stated incorrectly.

Serious factual inaccuracies include the claim that the background of the famous title sequence to *Touch of Evil* (Orson Welles, 1958) was "designed for the credits". (35) While the authors refer to the relocation of the credit titles in the 1998 re-release version, they apparently fail to understand that rather than being the result of some recent butchery, the new cut strives to be faithful to Welles' original wishes, which explicitly opposed the placing of credits over the masterful long take with which the film opens. Particularly painful is their assertion that "Nowadays, the overwhelming majority of individuals who create title sequences for movies are credited. [...] That notwithstanding, none of them has ever appeared in an opening sequence." (291) The latter part of this claim is belied by opening credits reproduced in the authors' own book. (e.g. 197, 205, 251)

Since the book contains a considerable number of errors, one would be unwise to accept it as a consistently reliable source of factual data. The absence of any footnotes is deeply regrettable. A bibliography is supplied, but almost all the entries are citations of websites, in which only the site name and home page (but not article titles, authors, or even subjects) are provided. To refer the reader to www.google.es, for instance, is not remotely helpful. Indeed, there is virtually no acknowledgement of the historical discoveries or critical perspectives of other researchers in the field. The authors' characterisation of previous scholarship as having "avoided any work requiring research" is unjust; it is a claim one suspects they might not have made had their own secondary research been more rigorous. (254)

While Solana and Boneu's written account is far from perfect, students and other researchers should nevertheless be grateful for their not-inconsiderable achievements. Although an increasing amount of scholarly effort has been devoted to the subject of title sequences in the past few years, this is the most sustained account published to date in the English language. The stills alone more than justify the cover price, and an added bonus is the accompanying DVD-ROM containing QuickTime copies (of variable quality) of more than one hundred aptly chosen title sequences. The rights-holders are, ironically, uncredited, so we must give thanks for the apparent laxity of Spanish copyright laws, which have allowed a far more extensive reproduction of film sequences and stills than would be financially viable in many other countries. And so, despite its manifold faults, I must advise all fans of film title sequences to seek out a copy of *Uncredited* at the first opportunity.

First published in *Design and Culture,* vol. 1, no. 1, March 2009, 135–36. DOI: 10.2752/175470709787375805.

BOOK REVIEW: SAUL BASS: A LIFE IN FILM AND DESIGN

By Jennifer Bass and Pat Kirkham
London: Laurence King Publishing, 2011

Fans of Saul Bass have eagerly anticipated this much delayed book since its first announcement around ten years ago. It's been a long wait, but the result does not disappoint. Edited, complied, and designed by his daughter, Jennifer, and written by Pat Kirkham, Professor in the History of Design, Decorative Arts, and Culture at the Bard Graduate Centre in New York, this stunningly produced collaboration is a treasure trove of top-quality visual material, contextual history, first-person accounts, and incisive critical observations.

Bass is already celebrated as one of the foremost designers of the twentieth century, and has gained particular recognition for his groundbreaking film title sequences, posters, and advertisements, as well as a string of iconic corporate logos. Yet his work in these fields accounts for only a portion of his astonishingly varied and prolific output. In a career spanning more than fifty years, he has fulfilled commissions for commercials, product packaging, book covers, album covers, exhibitions, and even service stations. Doing justice to the full scope of his undertakings, this book is bound to augment his already considerable reputation, as well as that of his wife, Elaine, whom Kirkham takes pains to credit for her contributions to their many collaborative projects.

A foreword by film director Martin Scorsese, for whom Saul and Elaine designed four title sequences, is followed by two chapters outlining his career development. Five further chapters centre (sometimes loosely) on his work in specific design fields, from film titling to corporate identity. The range and organisation of content is varied and stimulating. Kirkham explains, "I am interested in telling history through many voices, including reminiscences, images and anecdotes, as well as more obviously academic and analytical modes, and have included commentaries other than my own. Saul's 'voice' runs through this text, not least because he loved to tell stories." (viii) It is a felicitous choice.

The heart of the book is its images (close to one and a half thousand in all). Most illustrate Bass's work, using reproductions of his two-dimensional designs, frame stills from his films and motion graphics, and photographs of his other projects, but the many portrait shots are an added pleasure. All the images are judiciously chosen and presented; some occupy a full page or double spread, with others (especially the title sequence graphics) laid out in series that capture the development and flavour of his more complex works. For instance, his animated epilogue to *Around the World in 80 Days* (Michael Anderson, 1956) is described in a sequence of thirty-three frame stills. Although the images are captivating in their own right, the extensive history and commentaries illuminate them still further.

Some images, such as film posters, will already be familiar to many readers, but a wealth of previously unpublished material is also included. This ranges from preliminary sketches and abandoned ideas (which provide fascinating insights into Bass's creative process) to completed items never intended for wide publication, such as party invitations and stationery. Even in a book of this size, it is impossible to feature all his work—I was sorry that his immensely enjoyable title sequence for *That's Entertainment, Part II* (Gene Kelly, 1976) only earned a footnote—but the range and abundance of what is included more than compensates for the omissions.

The only infelicity of the book is that the authors present some of Bass's work in slightly puzzling order. In particular, Chapter Five, which deals with his return to film titling in the last years of his life, feels premature. The structural difficulties appear to stem from the authors' uncertainty about the relative merits of addressing Bass's work thematically or chronologically. However, the scope of his assignments, and the assorted media in which he worked during long, overlapping periods probably makes this unavoidable, and, in any case, the book is so informative and enjoyable that it hardly matters.

Saul Bass assembled much of the book's material himself while writing an unfinished memoir. By collaborating with Kirkham, Jennifer Bass sought to "honor [his] original vision, but within a new, more complete context". (xi) The result is a triumph, and the publisher's claim to offer "the definitive treatment of this great American designer and filmmaker" is no empty boast. There is more that can be said, of course, and future books may usefully do just that, but I am unable to imagine that any single volume will supplant this one as the superlative reference work on Bass. A must-have for anyone interested in graphic design, it is certain to delight his followers and astonish newcomers in equal measure.

First published in *Design and Culture,* vol. 4, no. 3, November 2012, 394–96. DOI: 10.2752/175470812X13361292229636.

BOOK REVIEW:
SAUL BASS: ANATOMY OF FILM DESIGN

By Jan-Christopher Horak
Lexington, KY: University Press of Kentucky, 2014

In Saul Bass's Oscar-winning short film, *Why Man Creates* (1968), an animated snail muses, "Have you ever thought that radical ideas threaten institutions, then become institutions and in turn reject radical ideas which threaten institutions?" "No!" replies a second snail, to which the first responds, "Gee, for a minute I thought I had something!"

This humorous exchange might be read as an apt comment on the trajectory of Bass's own career, as Horak observes. Having started out designing print advertisements in the 1940s, in the mid-1950s Bass diversified into creating film title sequences. His startlingly modernistic approach to titling brought him celebrity and inspired a great deal of copycat work. Wearied by the ubiquity of the new norms he had played such a role in creating, in the mid-1960s Bass almost entirely withdrew from titling work, returning only to produce a handful of highly acclaimed sequences in his final years. Instead, as Bass's motion work gravitated toward short films, the philosophy of creativity, its origins, and its modes of consumption would become an explicit area of focus in his cinematic musings.

Although Bass found success in a wide range of design fields, with the bulk of his output falling under the loose umbrella of commercial art, today his name remains most intrinsically associated with film title sequences and with those posters, for films such as *Vertigo* (Alfred Hitchcock, 1958), that shared their iconography. Jan-Christopher Horak's important new publication does justice to these celebrated projects—providing new insights in what might already seem a well-trodden field. At the same time, his extended analysis of Bass's other motion work, including television adverts, six short films (1964–1983), and the sci-fi fiction feature, *Phase IV* (1974), makes an extremely valuable contribution to an area that has hitherto been largely overlooked in both popular and scholarly writings about Bass.

As Director of the UCLA Film and Television Archive, whose previous studies range from American avant-garde cinema to Hollywood movie marketing, Horak is admirably qualified to offer an original, informed, and rounded analysis. Couching his arguments within a series of pertinent contexts, he presents Bass not as an unaccountable genius but rather as an outlier, whose career is best understood as that of a canny exploiter of industrial structures and needs (especially those of the Hollywood studio system and multinational corporate sponsors). He proposes, moreover, that the ways Bass came to fulfil those needs were shaped by his grasp of the opportunities offered by time and place (mid-century New York City) to develop his appreciation of emergent schools of modern art and to apply their logic and aesthetics within the burgeoning field of commercial design. Bass, he argues, "carved out a lifelong career by draping himself in that European modernist mantle, but with a romantic American touch, and then selling that aesthetic to the Hollywood entertainment industry as a form of moral uplift". (353)

Much of Horak's source material is taken from the extensive Bass Collection of the Academy of Motion Picture Arts and Sciences, which includes internal company memos as well as unfinished and unused designs. He supplements this with interviews and correspondence he conducted with more than a dozen of Bass's colleagues and friends. Combined with his own considerable knowledge of twentieth-century art history and of the mid-century American film and design industries, these various components lend credence to the multi-layered personal readings he later elaborates in a series of exquisitely close studies of Bass's work.

Drawing on both interviews and archive resources, a striking and useful argument Horak lays out in his introduction and opening chapter serves the double purpose of encouraging readers to reflect on their current understanding of Bass and his work and of ratifying the author's own approach. Describing the level of control exercised by the Bass studio in the development of its brand, Horak shows how carefully the flow of interview material and images offered to newspapers and journals was managed, further noting the rejection of early manuscripts for a long-cherished 'official' book. As well as providing a fascinating insight into the extent to which Bass has been the author of his own myth, it is also a cautionary tale of how such control shaped journalese within the designer's lifetime and continues to influence popular and academic writing alike.

Although the organisation of chapters traces a loosely chronological and formal journey from poster and title design through to short stand-alone films and, finally, *Phase IV*, Horak regularly deviates from this path. "If we can identify consistencies in the Bass style, design motifs, and brand", he argues, "then we can begin to read the designer's work in its specific historical context—its moment in history—as well as understand how it speaks to the contemporary generation, spawning countless homages and imitations". (92) Locating such consistencies by studying the repetition and variation of styles and themes across different media proves both fascinating and fruitful.

The ways in which Horak does so are informed, to a high degree, by exactly the kinds of art theory of which Bass was often vocally dismissive. One of his critical strengths is that instead of contenting himself by lazily name-checking schools and individuals (Constructivism, Bauhaus, Picasso, Mondrian, Modigliani) as some lesser Bass pundits have done, he conducts his formal analysis with a rigor that helps elucidate the inner logic of the work. The comparisons he draws with other art and artists are invariably enhanced by his diligent examination and description of Bass's own compositional strategies. Nor are his references confined to visual art, as his structural analysis of the titles for *Something Wild* (Jack Garfein, 1961) demonstrates. These are, he observes, "among the most mathematically precise of Bass's career. The 2:45-minute title sequence is exactly divided into three sections of 65 seconds, 65 seconds, and 35 seconds [...]. The proportions conform almost exactly to Gustav Freitag's triangle of dramatic structure for a five-act play, which is in turn derived from Plato's concept of the Golden Proportion: exposition, rising action, climax, falling action, dénouement." (245–46)

The material centred on Bass's six short films—*The Searching Eye* (1964); *From Here to There* (1964); *Why*

Man Creates (1968); *Notes on the Popular Arts* (1978); *The Solar Film* (1980); and *Quest* (1983)—and the feature-length *Phase IV* make an especially useful contribution to critical appreciation and understanding of the designer's work. There is little prior scholarship in this area, and it is to be hoped that Horak's study will help to raise the lesser-known titles from their current relative obscurity.

Ambitious, wide-ranging, diligent, and consistently interesting, *Saul Bass: Anatomy of Film Design* should be considered essential reading for any Bass scholar or enthusiast. Designed to please lay and academic readerships alike, Horak's style is for the most part pretty accessible (although some readers may find he occasionally overestimates their prior knowledge of art theories and theorists). The book's greatest weakness, as Horak is no doubt painfully aware, is its paucity of images. His forty-five rather murky monochrome illustrations (only thirty-seven of which feature Bass's work) compare poorly with the 1,484 illustrations (1,234 in colour) featured in Jennifer Bass and Pat Kirkham's 'official' publication, *Saul Bass: A Life in Film and Design* (2011). Nevertheless, the detail and intelligence of Horak's writing ensures the value of his book as a companion piece to that earlier volume, which it both complements and supplements.

First published in *Journal of Film and Video*, vol. 68, no. 2, summer 2016, 61–62. DOI: 10.5406/jfilmvideo.68.2.0061.

WORKS CITED

Abel, Richard. *The Ciné Goes to Town: French Cinema 1896–
1914*, Revised Edition (London: University of California
Press, 1998).

Allison, Deborah. *Promises in the Dark: Opening Title
Sequences in American Feature Films of the Sound Period*,
(PhD diss., University of East Anglia, 2001).

Andrews, Mallory. "*Nothing Sacred* (1937)", *Art of the Title*,
18 July 2017. www.artofthetitle.com/title/nothing-sacred.

Barr, Charles. "CinemaScope and After", in Gerald Mast and
Marshall Cohen (eds.), *Film Theory and Criticism* (New
York: Oxford University Press, 1974), 120–46.

Bass, Jennifer, and Pat Kirkham. *Saul Bass: A Life in Film
and Design* (London: Laurence King Publishing, 2011).

Bass, Saul. "The 'Compleat Film-Maker'—from Titles to
Features", *American Cinematographer*, vol. 58, no. 3,
March 1977, 288–91, 325–27.

Bazin, André. "A Little Late", *Velvet Light Trap*, no. 21, summer
1985, 15–16.

———. "The End of Montage", *Velvet Light Trap*, no. 21,
summer 1985, 14–15.

Belton, John. "CinemaScope: The Economics of Technology",
Velvet Light Trap, no. 21, summer 1985, 35–43.

————. *Widescreen Cinema* (Cambridge, Mass.: Harvard University Press, 1992).

Big Film Design. www.bigfilmdesign.com (accessed 24 March 2003; quoted content now discontinued).

Billanti, Dean. "The Names Behind the Titles", *Film Comment*, vol. 18, no. 3 (1982), 60–71.

Blackburn, Dick. "Opening Flourish", *Guardian* (London): *The Guide*, 17 February 1996, 4–5.

Bordwell, David. "Widescreen Aesthetics and Mise en Scene Criticism", *Velvet Light Trap*, no. 21, summer 1985, 18–25.

Bordwell, David, and Kristin Thompson. *Film Art: An Introduction* (New York: Alfred A. Knopf, 1986).

Bordwell, David, Janet Staiger, and Kristin Thompson. *The Classical Hollywood Cinema: Film Style and Mode of Production to 1960* (London: Routledge, 1985).

Bradshaw, Peter. "*Catch Me if You Can*", *Guardian* (London): *Review*, 31 January 2003. https://www.theguardian.com/culture/2003/jan/31/artsfeatures4.

Branco, Sergio Dias. "The Mosaic-Screen: Exploration and Definition", *Refractory*, vol. 14, December 2008. http://refractory.unimelb.edu.au/2008/12/27/the-mosaic-screen-exploration-and-definition-%E2%80%93-sergio-dias-branco.

Brooke, Eliza. "How to Capture the Feeling of a Movie in a Single Font", *Vox*, 12 November 2018. https://www.vox.com/the-goods/2018/11/12/18071808/suspiria-sorry-to-bother-you-the-favourite-title-design.

Brookey, Robert, and Jonathan Gray. "'Not Merely Para': Continuing Steps in Paratextual Research", *Critical Studies in Media Communication*, vol. 34, no. 2 (2017), 101–110.

Brooks, Karen, Gideon Bosker, and Reed Darmon. *Atomic Cocktails: Mixed Drinks for Modern Times* (San Francisco: Chronicle Books, 1998).

Buscombe, Ed (ed.). *BFI Companion to the Western* (London: BFI/Andre Deutsch, 1991).

Buscombe, Ed. "*The Hi-Lo Country*", *Sight & Sound*, vol. 9, no. 8, August 1999, 44–45.

Cawelti, John G. *The Six-Gun Mystique*, Second Edition

(Bowling Green: Bowling Green State University Popular Press, 1984).

CBS News. "Giving Credit: The Creators of Movie Title Sequences", *CBS News*, 26 February 2017. https://www.cbsnews.com/news/giving-credit-the-creators-of-movie-title-sequences/.

Central Station Art. *"The Killer Inside Me* Titles", *Vimeo*, 8 May 2013. https://vimeo.com/65785680.

Charney, Leopold Joseph. *Just Beginnings: Film Studies, Close Analysis and the Viewer's Experience* (Ann Arbor: UMI, 1993).

Combs, Richard. "*High Noon*", *Monthly Film Bulletin*, vol. 53, no. 629, June 1986, 186–87.

Cooper, Texas Jim. "Tex Ritter: His Songs and Personality Expressed the Ethos of our West", *Films in Review*, vol. 24, no. 4, April 1970, 204–16.

Crowther, Bosley. *"The Pink Panther"*, *New York Times*, 24 April 1964, 25.

Directors Guild of America. "Possessory Credit Timeline", *DGA Quarterly*, February 2004. https://www.dga.org/Craft/DGAQ/All-Articles/0402-Feb-2004/Possessory-Credit-Timeline.aspx.

Doty, Alexander. "Music Sells Movies: (Re)new(ed) Conservatism in Film Marketing", *Wide Angle*, vol. 10, no. 2 (1988), 70–79.

Dowdy, Andrew. *The Films of the Fifties: The American State of Mind* (New York: William Morrow, 1973).

Eisner, Lotte H. *Fritz Lang* (London: Secker and Warburg, 1976).

Elley, Derek. "Epic Entertainment", *The Movie*, vol. 4, chapter 41, 803–06.

English, T.J. "Martin Scorsese on Framing", *Blank on Blank*, 12 August 2016. https://allarts.org/programs/blank-on-blank/blank-blank-scorsese/.

Finler, Joel W. *The Hollywood Story* (New York: Crown Publishers, 1988).

French, Philip. *"Catch Me if You Can"*, *Observer*, 2 February 2003. https://www.theguardian.com/film/2003/feb/02/

philipfrench.

Fuchs, Cynthia. *"Auto Focus"*, *Nitrate Online*, 22 November 2002. https://nitrateonline.com/2002/rautofocus.html.

Fuller, Graham. *"High Noon"*, *The Movie*, vol. 5, chapter 53, 1052–53.

Geffner, David. "First Things First", *Filmmaker Magazine*, vol. 6, no. 1, fall 1997. https://www.filmmakermagazine.com/archives/issues/fall1997/firstthingsfirst.php.

Genette, Gerard. *Paratexts: Thresholds of Interpretation* (Cambridge: Cambridge University Press, 1997).

Gomery, Douglas. "Hollywood as Industry", in John Hill and Pamela Church Gibson (eds.), *American Cinema and Hollywood: Critical Approaches* (Oxford: Oxford University Press, 2000), 19–28.

Gómez Bernaus, Ana. "Type and Title Sequences: An Interview with Karin Fong", *Creative Cloud*, 11 May 2018. https://creativecloud.adobe.com/discover/article/type-and-title-sequences-an-interview-with-karin-fong.

Grainge, Paul. "Branding Hollywood: Studio Logos and the Aesthetics of Memory and Hype", *Screen*, vol. 45, no. 4, Winter 2004, 344–62.

Gray, Jonathan. *Show Sold Separately: Promos, Spoilers, and Other Media Paratexts* (New York: New York University Press, 2010).

Groucutt, Jonathan. "Scoring for the Sixties", *The Movie*, vol. 7, chapter 75, 1498–1500.

Gunning, Tom. "The Cinema of Attraction: Early Film, its Spectator and the Avant-Garde", *Wide Angle*, vol. 8, no. 3/4, fall 1986, 63–70.

Hardy, Phil (ed.). *The Aurum Film Encyclopedia: Horror* (London: Aurum Press, 1985).

Heffernan, Harold. "The Minstrel is the Man of the Hour", *Baltimore Sun*, 26 July 1953, 66.

Hill, Gladwin. "Screening the Movies' 'Main Titles'", *New York Times*, 7 June 1953, X4.

Hincha, Richard. "Selling CinemaScope: 1953–1956", *Velvet Light Trap*, no. 21, summer 1985, 44–53.

Horak, Jan-Christopher. *Saul Bass: Anatomy of Film Design*

(Lexington, KY: University Press of Kentucky, 2014).

Horstman, Dorothy. *Sing Your Heart Out, Country Boy* (Nashville: Country Music Foundation Press, 1975, 1996).

Jackson, Kevin (ed.). *Schrader on Schrader & Other Writings* (London: Faber and Faber, 1990).

James, David E. *Allegories of Cinema: American Film in the Sixties* (Princeton: Princeton University Press, 1989).

James, Nick. "Out of the Pastiche", *Sight & Sound*, vol. 13, no. 3, March 2003, 3.

Jenkins III, Henry. "Fifi was My Mother's Name!: Anarchistic Comedy, the Vaudeville Aesthetic, and *Diplomaniacs*", *Velvet Light Trap*, no. 27, fall 1990, 3–27.

Johnson, Grady. "Credits Ledger: Film Title-Making is Inventive Business", *New York Times*, 16 October 1955, X6.

Johnston, Keith M. *Coming Soon: Film Trailers and the Selling of Hollywood Technology* (Jefferson, N.C.: McFarland, 2009).

Kemp, Wolfgang. "The Narrativity of the Frame", in Paul Duro (ed.), *The Rhetoric of the Frame* (Cambridge: Cambridge University Press, 1996), 11–23.

Kirkham, Pat. "Looking for the Simple Idea", *Sight & Sound* vol. 4, no. 2, February 1994, 16–20.

Kitses, Jim. *Horizons West* (London: Thames and Hudson, 1969).

Kuntzel, Thierry. "The Film-Work, 2", *Camera Obscura*, no. 5, spring 1980, 6–69.

Lack, Russell. *Twenty Four Frames Under: A Buried History of Film Music* (London: Quartet Books, 1997).

LaSalle, Mick. "*Catch Me if You Can*", *San Francisco Chronicle*, 25 December 2002. https://sfgate.com/movies/ article/Holiday-Movies-Sit-back-and-enjoy-his-flight- 2743359.php.

Makal, Katie. "Digital Domain Animates *Fight Club* Titles", *Design in Motion*, 24 November 1999. http://DesigninMotion.com/.getarticle/.378231349 (accessed 1 September 2001; page now discontinued).

Mayersberg, Paul. *Hollywood the Haunted House* (Harmondsworth: Penguin Books, 1967).

McKay, Herbert C. *Amateur Movie Making* (New York: Falk Publishing, 1928).

McNab, Geoffrey. "*Catch Me if You Can*", *Sight & Sound*, vol. 13, no. 3, February 2003, 39–40.

Muschamp, Herbert. "Blueprint: The Shock of the Familiar", *New York Times Magazine*, 13 December 1998. https://www.nytimes.com/1998/12/13/magazine/blueprint-the-shock-of-the-familiar.html.

N.B. "Title Sequences in Film: A Deficit of Credits", *The Economist*, 25 January 2013. https://www.economist.com/prospero/2013/01/25/a-deficit-of-credits.

Neale, Steve, and Frank Krutnik. *Popular Film and Television Comedy* (London: Routledge, 1990).

Neale, Steve. *Genre and Hollywood* (London: Routledge, 2000).

New York Times. "Howard Da Silva Loses Film Credit", *New York Times*, 26 April 1951, 34.

———. "Those Theme Songs!", *New York Times*, 4 August 1929, A5.

Ouellette, Jennifer. "Credit Where Credit is Due", *Ars Technica*, 30 December 2019. https://arstechnica.com/gaming/2019/12/the-2010s-were-a-veritable-golden-age-of-opening-credits-in-television/.

Prendergast, Roy M. *Film Music: A Neglected Art* (New York: W. W. Norton, 1977).

Re, Valentina. "From Saul Bass to Participatory Culture: Opening Title Sequences in Contemporary Television Series", *NECSUS*, Spring 2016. https://necsus-ejms.org/saul-bass-participatory-culture-opening-title-sequences-contemporary-tv-series/.

Richardson, Lance. "Opening Act", *The Verge*, 5 July 2017. https://www.theverge.com/2017/7/5/15886698/tv-title-sequence-history-sopranos-american-gods-netflix-skip.

Robertson, Patrick. *Guinness Film Facts and Feats* (London: Guinness Books, 1985).

Robinson, David. *Georges Méliès: Father of Film Fantasy* (London: Museum of the Moving Image, 1993).

Rovin, Jeff. *The Signet Book of Movie Lists* (New York: NEL,

1979).

Saffari, Hilda. "The Most Iconic Movie Title Sequences of All Time. And Why They Work", *frame.io*, 4 June 2018. https://blog.frame.io/2018/06/04/iconic-movie-title-sequences/.

Salt, Barry. *Film Style and Technology: History and Analysis,* Second Edition (London: Starword, 1992).

Sanjek, Russell. *American Popular Music and its Business: The First Four Hundred Years—Volume III: From 1900–1984* (Oxford: Oxford University Press, 1988).

Seidman, Steve. *Comedian Comedy: A Tradition in Hollywood Film* (Ann Arbor: UMI Research Press, 1981).

Sellers, John. "TV's Golden Age of Opening Credits", *Salon*, 18 February 2012. https://www.salon.com/2012/02/18/tvs_golden_age_of_opening_credits/.

Shepter, Joe. "Imaginary Forces", *Adobe Motion Gallery.* www.adobe.co.uk/motion/gallery/imgforces/main.html (accessed 10 August 2005; page now discontinued).

Smith, Jeff. *The Sounds of Commerce: Marketing Popular Film Music* (New York: Columbia University Press, 1998).

Solana, Gemma, and Antonio Boneu. *Uncredited: Graphic Design and Opening Titles in Movies* (Barcelona: Index Book, 2007).

Spellerberg, James. "CinemaScope and Ideology", *Velvet Light Trap*, no. 21, summer 1985, 26–34.

Tanz, Jason. "How TV Opening Titles Got to Be So Damn Good", *Wired*, 23 March 2017. https://www.wired.com/2017/03/tv-opening-titles-got-damn-good/.

Theisen, Earl. "The Evolution of the Motion Picture Story, Part II", *The International Photographer,* vol. 8, no. 4 (1936), 12.

Thilk, Chris. "Movie Marketing Madness: *The Beguiled*", *Chris Thilk* (blog), 22 June 2017. https://christhilk.com/2017/06/22/the-beguiled-marketing/.

Thomson, David. "The Man with the Golden Pen", *Independent on Sunday* (London), 21 June 1998, 19–20.

Trav S.D. "On the Important Cultural Role Played by W. C. Frito", *Travalanche* (blog), 29 January 2015. https://travsd.wordpress.com/2015/01/29/on-the-important-cultural-role-played-by-w-c-frito.

Tylski, Alexandre (ed.). *Les Cinéastes et leurs génériques* (Paris: Editions L'Harmattan, 2008).

Warshow, Robert. "Movie Chronicle: The Westerner", in Gerald Mast and Marshall Cohen (eds.), *Film Theory and Criticism* (New York: Oxford University Press, 1974), 401–16.

Writers Guild of America. *Theatrical and Television Basic Agreement* (1995).

INDEX TO FILMS AND DESIGNERS

Printed in Great Britain
by Amazon

46983054R00129